S0-BDH-275

THE PLAINS BROOD ALONE

Barabaig tribesmen.

THE PLAINS BROOD ALONE

Tribesmen of the Serengeti

J. Birney Dibble, M.D.

ZONDERVAN PUBLISHING HOUSE
A DIVISION OF THE ZONDERVAN CORPORATION
GRAND RAPIDS, MICHIGAN

THE PLAINS BROOD ALONE

Library of Congress Catalog Card Number 72-85568

Printed in the United States of America

To: my father, whose consecrated life is the only inspiration I ever really needed

To: Miss Jean Mykelbust, who would have approved the paraphrasing of the prayer above her desk

To: Rev. Douglas Lundell, who taught us how to live before he died

Contents

Foreword

Once again I have returned from Africa, the gumbo-clay still on my shoes, and the eerie yowl of the hyena still haunting my pre-sleep dreams. And once again I have settled back into the same life — house, work, friends (a few have gone, out of this life or to some other place on earth) — and all over again I face the loneliness of civilization. For over a year I have again lived the life of a pioneer, and for adventure I did not need to read *Field and Stream* or the poems of Robert Service. Now I am home, whatever that means to a man with the call of the wild goose ringing in his ears.

Once again I remember the words:

> Can't you hear the Wild? — it's calling you.
> Let us probe the silent places,
>   let us seek what luck betide us;
> Let us journey to a lonely land I know.
> There's a whisper on the night-wind,
>   there's a star agleam to guide us,
> And the Wild is calling, calling, — let us go.*

I went to the lonely land, not the Yukon of which

* *The Call of the Wild* — Robert Service.

Service spoke, but to the lonely, brooding plains of Africa. Not to a cold white land, but to a warm land that is green half the year and brown half the year. And still a lonely land.

The trail was not unbroken before me, for after all there were still the faint footprints in the sand of Livingstone, the first medical missionary to Tanzania, and the prints still deep and clean of John Holt and Joe Norquist, of Denny Lofstrom and Ken Wilcox and Don Rude, all medical missionaries to Tanzania. There were even a few faint prints on the track that I recognized as my own, made four years before. I tried to follow my footprints and found that they didn't always lead to the same places that they had during the one and a half years I had spent out there before. But they did lead back to Kiomboi, and I lived there again for another year and a half.

This book is not written to describe the practice of medicine in a rural African hospital, since I have already done this.* Also, I don't want to convey a travelogue picture of Tanzania like a somewhat longish brochure on the tourist attractions of this "fabulous land of wild animals and Masai *morans*." I do not want just to take you on a boring guided tour of the buildings at the Kiomboi Lutheran Hospital where I spent the better part of three years. But I do want to place that hospital in the greater context of a country struggling to find its way in the world. That hospital, with its surrounding peoples, presents in microcosm many of the problems which beset the country of Tanzania. Represented there were the educated Africans, peasants, government leaders, day laborers, students, missionaries, primitive tribesmen, nomads, Christians and Muslims and animists, teachers and preachers and nurses. Present also were the pressures and the stimuli

* For a more detailed look at the everyday life of a missionary doctor in Africa, the reader is referred to the author's book, *In This Land of Eve* (Abingdon, 1965).

which make people act, react, and abreact: religion, politics, witchcraft, iconoclasm, reactionism, revolution, education, rules and regulations of man and God.

What I really want to do is introduce you to some of the people I knew, and take you, in your imagination at least, on a non-tourist trip or two. I do want to describe the physical setup at Kiomboi Hospital, and I want the reader to be aware of some of the problems we faced there, but these are included in the last chapter solely to give the reader the perspective I had when I sat down to write this book.

For Tanzania is many things to many people. The vast expanses of grasslands in the Serengeti. The University at Dar es Salaam. The mission hospital at Kiomboi. The big towns of Arusha and Moshi. The farmer on his three acres of sandy soil. All these scenes are Tanzania, and at any given moment, in any given place, one can say "*This* is Tanzania." And if one confines himself for too long to any one of these situations he will soon forget that there is any other Tanzania. The tourist, the student, the doctor or nurse, the sports-hunter, and all the others to be seen in profile in the following pages will tell you a different story if you ask them, "What is Tanzania?"

So to whom do you listen?

All of them.

Introduction

There was, of course, a pervasive nostalgia about returning to Africa. We could all feel it, children and parents alike. Shortly after we arrived the dry season ended, and one afternoon during a storm I sat down at my desk and tried to capture in a few brief words the emotions that assailed us.

It was on a day just like this, four years ago, that I sat at a desk, not this desk but a similar one only a few hundred yards away, and wrote the last chapter of a book that itself had not yet been written. Then the rains beat on the metal roof as they do now, and I was soon to leave that desk and that home, to leave my friends of a year and a half on the plateau of Irambaland in the deep heart of Africa. And to return to my own home and my own people in the heartland of America, where I was to work as before – but no, not as before, but with a longing for Irambaland reverberating within me like the drums from the village of Kiomboi.

Now the rains have come again, strong and white from the black clouds overhead, drilling the dry sands with sustenance, beating the blazing red *pori* flowers we planted years ago by the tree near our house. The thunder rolls, and the dry riverbeds run with water, and the children run from window to window with cries of glee, watching the little rivulets become wide streams as they rush past our house in the sandy paths to the church and to the hospital.

We have been here four days. It is as if we had never left. The people are the same, some with different faces, but the same people nevertheless. Warm smiles of welcome. Olive's sheets on our bed. Alice's dishes in our cabinets. Inez's flowers in our dining room and living room. Gideon Jumbe's children playing in our garden. Eliasafi Ndemsumburo's hand in mine. Nathaniel Msambe's help on the wards.

And above all, the open, trusting looks of the patients on the wards. "I have come to you," their faces say, "for help. I don't care where you come from, and I don't care when you leave, as long as you are here now, for tomorrow might be too late. Help me now."

These feelings were to prevail throughout our stay, although blunted in their sharpness by some of the events about which I will write. All the more reason to record them now.

The hospital had changed. During our absence an entirely new building had been erected, having been completed just a year before our return and formally dedicated by Tanzanian President Julius Nyerere. We therefore had a very modern physical plant, with two matching operating rooms, a separate labor ward, a large outpatient dispensary with private consultation rooms for the medical assistants who examined the 800-1200 patients who came daily, six patient wards, and a large connected unit for laundry, kitchens, and sterilizers. The hospital floors were of terrazo, with tiling four feet up the walls, and the wards had windows all around so that light and fresh air were not the problem they had been in parts of the old hospital.

The better sections of the old hospital were used for TB and leprosy clinics, for storage, and for office space which was at a premium before.

Most of the key positions on the staff were filled with qualified African personnel: assistant administrator, operating room supervisor, obstetrical supervisor, head nurses, staff nurses, and so forth. Missionaries still held the jobs of head administrator, nursing school headmistress, and doctors, but only because there were no qualified people yet to fill those positions. The hospital had been designated a government hospital, which meant that a yearly grant was received from the central government, so that the patients received free treatment. But it was still a mission hospital and would remain so until July of 1970.

The hospital grounds were much the same. The roads had not been improved, although ditching had been done to allow for better drainage during the rains. Several new houses had been built to upgrade the living standards of the ever-increasing number of graduate nurses. Two bigger, newer generators had replaced the one old one so we had electricity daily from 7 A.M. to 10:45 P.M. except on Sundays, instead of just evenings and on the two surgery days. In fact, we now did surgery five days a week, more than doubling the number of operations.

Dr. Joe Norquist was gone and had been replaced first by Dr. Dick Finlayson, then Dr. Don Rude, the latter still there. Dr. Ken Wilcox, who had replaced me four years before, had just gone home a few months before we returned. Both Finlayson and Norquist left before their terms of service were up but not of their own volition. Don Rude therefore had been handling the work of the hospital alone for five months when I arrived at Kiomboi, an overwhelming task that I have discussed more fully in Chapter 13, "Hospitali ya Wamishoneri wa Kiomboi."

In the introduction to my book, *In This Land of Eve,*

I spoke of three dreams: "Dreams like that of Dr. Bob Jensen – a medical school in the cornfield which stretches from our perch on a ten-foot anthill to the slopes of Kilimanjaro. Or the dream of Pastor Bob Ward – a cross-topped church in the valley stretching from the Masai steppes to the Kindira Mountains, home of the primitive, nomadic, Wakindiga. Or the dreams of Joe Norquist and myself which we have sitting in the doctors' office at Kiomboi – a new hospital with a good X-ray machine, a new laboratory, and, more important, a renewed spirit of love and cooperation."

Those three dreams have been achieved. Bob Jensen's medical school is even now being built; it is called the Kilimanjaro Christian Medical Center, and it sits in the cornfield that we saw from our anthill. Bob Ward's church in Diga-land was built several years ago, and around it has grown up a village of permanent houses; fields and gardens supply food to the people so that they no longer roam the hills searching for food. Joe Norquist's hospital has been built; it has a new X-ray machine and a new laboratory.

The renewed spirit of love and cooperation? May I hedge a little and say that there is a *better* spirit there now than there was eight years ago when I first arrived on the scene? Part of this improvement has come from the fact that there is less of the feeling that Kiomboi Lutheran Hospital is just a foreigner's mission hospital, administrated and controlled by foreign personnel. Now the hospital has come under the control of the Tanzanian people themselves, and many of the top positions are held by Tanzanians. Late in the year 1969 the first African doctor joined the staff.

So things are happening. Unborn dreams are being born and the infant dreams are maturing. This is true of the country at large also, and since Kiomboi does not exist in a vacuum, let us meet some of the people who live and work in present-day Tanzania.

The Plains Brood Alone

I've driven those roads on the ridges
 and watched the sun fighting the clouds
With its gold-yellow-orange-white switches
 that make the dark sky cry aloud.
And I've looked at the storm clouds a-rolling
 with lightning that shimmers and streaks
Down valleys that never have endings,
 up mountains that zoom to the peaks.
I've stood on the jagged escarpments
 where silently earth meets the sky
And satisfied many a longing
 and answered many a "why?"

The Plains of Wembere are open:
 I've seen them in all of their moods,
The antelope sleek in his wildness,
 the lioness roaming for food.
I've stood on a ten-foot high ant-hill
 that shone with a coppery red
While the graceful impala stood frozen
 with a spiralling crown on his head.
And far 'cross the vastness that stuns you,
 throwing dust in the blistering sky,
Flies a thundering huddle of zebras
 with a noise like a storm rushing by.

During six months of dryness you wonder
 if ever the life can return
To grasses and bushes and rivers,
 to flower, to thorntree, to fern.
The swamps are like endless dry deserts,
 the waterfowl long since have gone,
The waterholes lie cracked and empty,
 the game herds have all wandered on.

Then gradually the thunderheads gather,
increasingly closer each day,
And finally the skies break asunder
and finally the clouds have their way.
Now rivulets run into rivers
and rivers run on toward the sea.
The life-giving water is boundless
and life for the living is free.

I've wondered what manner of power
could resurrect life from the sod
And I've come to the final conclusion
that somehow there must be a God.
How else could all this have meaning,
why else should the plains brood alone,
How else could the rivers run rampant
and cause mountains to shudder and moan?

The manner of man's own undoing
has seldom if ever been clear
For does he not stand in the cyclone
and fly to the moon without fear?
He's learned how to harness the atom
and transmit his voice through the air
Yet somehow he's failed to remember
the God-given power of prayer.
The whole of mankind should have access
to the world that the Turus behold
As they stand on the Plains of Wembere
while the wonders of God's world unfold.

Then the manner of man's own undoing
would suddenly seem well-defined:
He has bridled the freedom of nature
and hemmed in its free-ranging mind
With high-rising walls of white concrete,
restrictions on body and soul.
He feeds well the fires of ferment,
he holds fast on a wandering goal.
But let Man look out on the long plains –
they'll welcome him back with a sigh.
Yes, the Plains of Wembere are open;
let Man see them clear ere he die.

THE PLAINS BROOD ALONE

A typical member of the tribe to which
Asha and his parents belonged.

1 / Asha Gidanje

Elizabeti's eyes were twin mirrors of the horror she had seen. The lids were drawn up, exposing the whites in a perfect circle around her black pupils. Her mouth quivered as she blurted out in Swahili, her English temporarily and completely forgotten, "A new patient, doctor, to be seen out of turn."

She stepped aside and quickly pointed the way into my small examining room. First came a tall, brown-clad Baraband. He spoke not a word, but stood impassively against the wall, feet widespread in their tire-soled sandals. His wife and child followed, she carrying the boy in such a way that I could see only the right side of his face.

Unable to discern the reason for Elizabeti's terrified appearance, I glanced at her again and found her staring directly at the child from the other side of the room.

"*Shida gani . . .*" I started to say. (What kind of trouble . . . .) But just then the mother turned around to show me the other side of the boy's face. If my physical body did not recoil at the sight, my mind certainly did. For the little boy *had* no left side of his face.

It had happened a week before.

The family's home was in the Yaida Valley, thirty miles from Kiomboi. Their *boma* – a circle of small wattle houses with a corral of dried thorn bushes – stood a half mile from its closest neighbor. To the east was the escarpment of Mbulu-land, and to the west the hills of the Wakindiga. The valley stretched away to the north as far as the eye could see, and if one cared to walk the length of it he would come eventually to the Ngorongoro Crater. And in the south were the mountains of Isanzu.

As the late afternoon sun crept down to the ridgeline, little Asha's father drove his cattle into the *boma* for safekeeping during the moonless night. But one obstreperous young bull was not to be hemmed in without a fight, and, throwing up his heels in battle he knocked the father to the ground, tore a hole through the *boma* and was gone. The father chased after him, caught him, and drove him viciously back to the *boma.* Tired, hot, and thirsty, he retired to his own hut and called for food and drink.

"Aren't you going to fix the hole in the fence?" the mother asked with some alarm.

"Oh, throw a log across it, just enough so the cows don't get out. I'll fix it in the morning." He began eating without another word, and his wife went to do his bidding.

She and two other wives dragged a log across the courtyard to the damaged wall of thornbushes and heaved it up onto the pile. It would do to keep the cattle in.

Darkness came. Total darkness, for the moon would not be up for several hours. The flickering campfire threw dancing shadows across the hard-packed mud of the *boma,* low voices recounted the events of the day, and before long the Barabaigs went off to their little huts to sleep. Eight-year-old Asha and his mother were the last to go for she had to rake up the coals into a tall neat pile so that some would still be live when the cold morning came. Already Asha was shivering a little, his slender little body wrapped snugly with a warm robe against the wind that blew steadily across the plain.

A hyena whooped its lonely hunting cry, and was soon joined in chorus by others. In the middle distance a lion roared, deep-voiced and menacing, perhaps driving a herd of zebras into the waiting arms of his queen. A nightbird cruised around the boma, its cry a high-pitched "plink," like a steel spike driven into concrete; endlessly it circled. The carnivores were abroad and the herbivores tensed for the long night.

The *boma* was deserted except for Asha, crouching before the dying embers. His mother, only a few yards away, was kneeling inside her hut, spreading smooth the skins on which they would sleep. Two glowing red eyes appeared at the new gap in the thornbush. If Asha had turned only a little to his left, or if his mother had come out for him only a moment earlier, the hyena would not have come loping across the court. His powerful jaws gaped, his shoulders hunched, his weak hind legs drove him steadily toward his objective.

Instinct, or a sudden observance of motion, or perhaps chance alone, caused Asha to jerk his head sideways just as the *fici* (pronounced "fee-see") struck. This movement alone saved him from being dragged by the head out of the *boma,* into the night, from which there would be no return. In retrospect, maybe it would have been better.

The jaws snapped shut. A terrifying scream tore the soft night air asunder.

Asha's mother looked up too late to save the boy from having his face ripped apart by fangs more powerful than even the lion or the leopard or the cheetah. She screamed *"Fici!"* but it was too late. Scurrying through the slit in the *boma*-wall the witch of the night was gone, and with him the now-defiled spirit of the boy Asha.

As I studied the wound, I talked with the father since the mother knew no Swahili. Actually the father knew little of the language but I could piece together the story all too well.

For several days after the *fici* had come, the wisest heads of the clan debated the fate of the child. Physical disfigurement to a Barabaig means much more than it does to you and me. It is a catastrophe that requires purification, even total ostracism from the tribe.* In the end, it was decided that if restoration of the face could be done by the *daktari* at the *Hospitali ya Wa-mishoneri,* the boy might be spared total ostracism from the clan, which of course for a boy so young would mean certain and sudden death as soon as the first night fell.

We did the first operation that same afternoon, cutting away the dead tissue and bone, the eye, the left cheek and lips, clearing away the rotting flesh in preparation for our attempts at restoration. It was a cruel job and I didn't sleep well that night.

I shall not detail the weeks that followed except to say that the remaining tissues threw down a base upon which we could build a new face. We swung "tube grafts," long tubes of skin, from back to neck and then up onto the gaping hole in the face itself. We knew that it would be a months-long job, perhaps a year or more, and we weren't any too sure what it would look like when we were finished. We never found out.

The father and mother stayed with the child constantly. The father cradled the boy in his arms by day,

* Readers of *In This Land of Eve* will remember the story of the woman who lived for eighteen years alone in the bush, after losing part of her leg from a burn.

and slept with him by night. The mother made *uji* and *ugale* and painstakingly spooned it into the unbandaged corner of his mouth. It was a sight to tear out one's heart.

The child Asha never overcame his fear of us. As we made rounds on the ward, coming closer and closer to his bed, his eye followed us, wide and staring. He never cried nor did he ever smile. He squirmed a little in his father's arms as we changed the bandages, but he didn't flinch away. He was like a little animal that knew we were trying to help him.

That eye follows me as I write these words. Fearful yet trusting. Akin to all the people I have ever treated. Symbolic now of the eye of the African as he studies what the white man will do next. I am me, he says. Can you help me, and teach me, and heal me, and work beside me, and still withal let me be *me?*

Then, one day, the child was gone. I saw his empty bed across the room as I started rounds on Ward C. Was it unusually quiet in the room? Were the medical assistants and nurses abnormally attentive to my orders? Was the child just outside with his parents, not yet come in this morning?

Finally I asked, "*Asha ni wapi?*" (Where is Asha?)

"*Amekwenda.*" (He has gone.)

"*Amekwenda?*"

"*Ametupwa porini,*" Marko Shila said softly, his eyes on the floor.

Ametupwa porini. (He has been thrown out into the bush.)

"*Kwa sababu gani?*" I asked. (For what reason?) I could feel the blood rush to my face, uncontrolled.

"Because," Mr. Shila continued in Swahili, "his father and mother were disappointed in the way the boy's face looks. They had thought that we might be able to perform some magic and restore the face to normal. They had begun to see lately that he would never look normal again. So rather than see him suffer longer, and then have to be put out in the bush anyway, they decided to get it over with."

Cool, clear, cruel logic. The African is nothing if he is not pragmatic. If you see that something is inevitable, bow to it. If it must be done, do it. If Asha must die anyway, why prolong it? Get it over with, and save the time, trouble, pain, and expense.

So in the dark of the night, when all the other patients were sleeping, and the nurse was busy elsewhere, Asha was gently lifted from the bed, cradled lovingly in his father's arms, taken out into the bush far from human habitation, and placed carefully on the ground. The father and mother walked softly into the forest toward their half-forgotten *boma,* midway between the lands of the Wambulu and the Wakindiga, the full moon lighting their path, the eerie howl of a prowling hyena sounding mournfully in the bush.

The Barabaig are "brown-skinned, tall, lean, graceful, and handsome."

2 / Malan

Asha Gidanje was a member of the primitive Barabaig tribe. His people represent one view of Tanzania which rarely comes to light in this modern day and you will even hear that it is no longer a true picture of Africa. Nevertheless it is still there, whether or not the leaders will acknowledge it, whether or not the tourist sees it, whether or not it will last much longer. This view is of the primitive tribes which live far from urban areas, their lives and customs unchanged for decades, perhaps for centuries. Neither the Germans nor the British tried very hard to make inroads into their culture, and what little they did was thwarted quickly and incisively by the tribes themselves.

One such tribe is the Barabaig, who, with their close relatives the Masai, are descended from peoples who migrated southward from Egypt centuries ago. They are, therefore, not black Africans (Bantu) but Nilo-hamites. They are brown-skinned, tall, lean, graceful, and handsome. Like the Masai, the men dress in brown robes draped loosely around their bodies, and the women wear the skins of cows, intricately beaded and smelling violently of the cow's urine with which they are cured. They are a pastoral people, owning huge herds of cattle. Their culture is patriarchal, polygamous, primitive. The elders of the tribe have vigorously fought against education, but one by one the children are breaking away to mission and government schools, and a few to the towns to seek employment. But even these few almost always return to the clan from which they left, and go back to the old ways.

The government recently has decided to take a hand in modernizing the tribe and has met a stone wall of resistance. The government is primarily interested in reducing the intertribal killings which go on uninterruptedly month after month, but this is a difficult task because it is part of the ritual of a young man's passage from adolescence to manhood that he make a kill of a lion or an elephant or a man, and by far the easiest to kill is a man. He will be goaded by father and girlfriend until he makes a man of himself by making a kill. His father will refuse him food, his girlfriend will refuse him her favors, and his peers will refuse him their company until he has killed. He will then take a witness with him and ambush someone of another tribe, usually a Turu, and drive a spear into his back and then hack off his ears as proof of his triumph. Only then can he join in the affairs of the tribe as a man.

It is estimated that several hundred Turus are killed every year by Barabaig warriors, and they have deserved the designation which other tribes have given them: "Mang'ati," the enemy. Recently, after a Turu teacher was killed on his way home from his classroom, the government rounded up several hundred Barabaig young men, jailed them for three months in an attempt to find out who did the killing, then released them without any real solution to the crime. Now the government has decided that all Mang'ati will be placed in Family *(Ujamaa)* Villages in an attempt to regiment them and introduce them to the new socialist state. Rev. Hal Faust, who has worked with the Barabaig for ten years, says it will never work. He is probably right. They are a proud, stubborn people, who will just disappear from the villages and lose themselves in the bush from whence they came.

These people will not willingly give up their cherished traditions and customs. There is too much at stake: their entire culture is threatened. They ask, "Why should I not live as I want to – what is wrong with my customs – who has the right to deny me my freedom?"

I could tell you stories of their ritual murders and of their lion-hunts, but I think it would be more interesting to lighten their dark image with a story of a wedding. I spent an entire day in the *boma* of a new bride, although she wasn't there, and found the events so interesting and different that I must pass them on. I was especially taken with one old woman, nut-brown and wrinkled with age, who seemed to have an important role to play. And indeed she did, as we shall see.

She would have to be considered an old woman, and there were times when even she would agree. Like the day of the wedding. She felt *very* old that day, watching and participating in the dancing and ceremonies. The bride, Malan, looked so young, but the old woman had known her since she was a child and it had been at least five years since Malan began to throw off the evil in her blood (menstruation). She herself had stopped that business four or five years before, so you can see she really was old.

Although she was not excluded from the dancing, no one would really have cared whether she was there or not except that all the married female relatives of both the groom and the bride were expected to be there, and of course she had very important duties to perform toward the end of the afternoon. People started coming early the morning of the wedding, almost before they got the groom safely out of the *boma* where he wouldn't be seen by the bride or anyone else. Actually, he lounged around a little way off by the wild fig tree where he had some honey-beer in a big tin. He also had a sick calf there which he tended from time to time; it died before the day was out.

All the women of the clan who were related in any way to the groom were there at the *boma* by the time the sun was overhead. Malan, of course, was hidden out in the bush; her big moment came the day before when she and all her unmarried female friends danced all day and walked singing through the forest all night. As dawn came, she was taken out into the wilderness a short distance from the *boma* and placed on a new cowskin and the women rubbed just a little red ochre onto her hair and arms.

Malan really was a beautiful girl, maybe not as tall and graceful as most of the Barabaig women, but with nice brown skin, not black like the Bantus all around. She had on a new dress of cowskin, the skirt and upper garment carefully cleaned and then soaked for weeks in cow's urine to soften it, and then worked with the teeth to render it almost like cloth. The dress was not decorated with beads, of course, because she was not yet married, but they rubbed enough ochre into it so that it was a reddish brown color. A few little children were left with her so she wouldn't be completely alone all day. She wouldn't actually be alone, of course, because their god Aseta would be with her.

The women of the bridegroom's family danced for several hours before the women of the bride's family arrived. They danced in pairs, one of them acting out the part of the bride, the other the groom, illustrating the various stages of the courtship and ending with the enactment of the consummation itself. Some of the younger women were extremely good at this and really worked themselves into a frenzy, chanting and singing and bouncing up and down. It was great fun. The outsider might be shocked by the dancing because it leaves nothing to the imagination. The jokes and banter that were tossed back and forth might have seemed lewd, but the revelers didn't consider them so. These are natural acts which have been given by Aseta for pleasure and should not be considered evil in themselves. At least that's the way they feel about it.

About halfway through the afternoon the scout on the roof of the house saw Malan's family coming. There were about fifty of them, all carrying gourds full of milk and grain and honey. They marched in a body across the drying grass, ignoring the path through the bush because they didn't want to walk single file. They were welcomed cordially and showed the room where they should place their gifts and they went in one by one and left them on the dirt floor. Then they were invited out to dance with the groom's womenfolk, and this dancing went on again until almost sundown.

The old woman grew very tired and spent most of the time in the circle around the dancers, chanting and rubbing her bracelets together to help keep time. For awhile she even took the shield and stick and beat time with them. All the time she kept thinking of that little girl out in the forest, waiting so patiently for her husband to claim her. Malan's free days were over. She would no longer romp with the children and roam the plains and forests with the girls, nor hide away in the forest glades with a lover. That was all done now.

For the first year she would be treated almost like a guest in the house, but after the year was over, she would be obliged to carry wood, fetch water, make *ugale*, bear children, and always be ready to submit to her husband on the nights he chose her over his other wives. And she would ache with jealousy when he ignored her for several nights in a row. She would listen intently, after the fires were out, and the children were quiet, to see if he would come, and if he didn't come, she would try to tell just where he went. But the old woman still envied Malan her youth, because it would be many years before she would feel the heart-ache of being ignored.

The dancing went on, then suddenly stopped: the ceremony of anointing with oil was due to begin. Half a dozen women were so honored, sisters and sisters-in-law of the bride, their heads piled high with the white butter-like stuff, which then dripped down onto their shoulders, most of it caught in a flat half-gourd held on the abdomen. Then they all went out of the *boma* and the anointed women smeared oil onto all parts of their bodies, taking off their clothes and rubbing the oil into their skins. They shared the excess with the rest so that they might partake of the blessings, and the old woman got a large handful and rubbed it into her clothes and up under her arms and between her legs. They laughed and joked as they helped each other cover themselves with the holy oil.

The sun was low on the hills lining their home valley when Malan's family left. Each received a big steaming gourd full of one of the favorite ceremonial foods—corn meal mush mixed with cow's milk and blood and cooked into a nice thick pudding. The gourds were tied onto their backs, and each received a new *fimbo* (walking stick), and they left, the white anointed heads among them shining beautifully in the waning light.

All the real fun was over, but the important part of the day was yet to come. It was almost dark when the old woman and another old crone went out to the hideaway in the forest to get Malan. She sat quietly on her cowskin, demurely covering her face with a brown cloth. One little baby was crying violently, but she ignored it, perhaps didn't even hear it. The other two children, only two to three years old, were wide-eyed, perhaps a little frightened by the falling darkness, wondering if they might have to stay there all night.

The old woman took the cloth from Malan's head and began working the thick ochre-colored butter into her hair so that it made a little red cap with an extension down the back of the neck. She was very careful to shape it beautifully, taking more time than really necessary because she wanted to calm Malan down a little. She could feel Malan trembling under her hands. She told Malan that her husband would be very strong and very gentle, and she need not worry about a thing. And as the old woman rubbed the ochre into Malan's clothes, and along her smooth-skinned legs, she told her he would treat her very kindly after they were married, and would never beat her unless she gave him cause, and even then he would not be cruel. You see, she knew him quite well.

Finally Malan was ready. The old woman helped her up and put the cow's halter around her neck and led her from the forest into the *boma* and into the newly built room where she would live the rest of her life. Then the halter was taken off and she went out of the *boma* to get her cooking stones and brought them back into her house. As she worked with them in the pitch blackness of her room, the old woman told her that her husband had never liked to wait for meals and would rightfully beat her if she were late. She also told her that she must always be sure to use a flaming stick to stir the milk because he loved the charcoal taste in the milk. As they talked, someone brought in a big cookpot, some cornmeal, and a burning firebrand from another part of the house. Malan ceremoniously began to cook the meal, but then as was their custom, the old woman grabbed the pot and ran laughing outside where another woman struck at her with some pieces of grass. She was acting the part of the bride being beaten by the husband for being late.

The old woman had one more duty to perform. She took a large gourd of butter and cowdung which she had collected fresh that morning, and took it into Malan's hut where she was patiently waiting. She lay Malan down on the cowskin mat where she would receive her husband, and the old woman lifted her skirt and carefully rubbed the dung onto her legs and between her thighs and over her buttocks, up to her navel, so that she was completely covered with this sweet smelling product of the revered cattle. All the while she was working, she told Malan of the greatness and goodness of her husband, how he was not only an important man now, but would someday be even greater. She told her she must never embarrass him, or be untrue to him, because he was too fine a man to be treated in that way.

And then at last, lying there in the total darkness of the night, Malan was ready to receive their husband, and the old woman stole off to her own room.

Women at a Barabaig wedding.

3/ Keja Makubi

Every culture builds up a storehouse of ideas, concepts and beliefs which become "available" for the people to utilize in the thought-processes which underlie their actions. For example, in Tanzania, tribal laws and mores have ruled the people for centuries. German and British colonialism presented new ideas to the people for about fifty years. An independent government now permeates every level of society with the teachings of socialism, self-reliance, and self-government. Animism is the religion of the majority and dictates much of their daily life. Christianity has been introduced and has won perhaps a million people to Christ. Islam has also been introduced and has won about a million people to Mohammed. Some tribes have no demonstrable religious beliefs, but even in these tribes there is always deference to a supernatural power of some kind even if it is simply a worship or reverence of ancestors. Education has become a driving force, taking up the time and energy of thousands of young people.

One could continue with an almost endless list of concepts which hold the minds of the people of Tanzania, and it can be demonstrated with statistics and books and newspaper articles that these concepts and ideas do indeed consume a great deal of the time of the individual. But if I were asked to name the one abstract idea that occupies more of the thought-life of the Tanzanian than any other, I would have great difficulty documenting my conclusion with those statistics, books, or newspaper articles. But I am convinced that the one overriding power in the life of the Tanzanian, in all walks of life and at all educational levels, is the fear of witchcraft.

Just talk with the patients in the hospital and ask them where they got their disease, or what happened that they injured themselves, and the overwhelming majority will tell you that they had been bewitched by someone or by something. Just go hunting anywhere and ask your African companion why he cut off the tail of the wildebeeste, and he will tell you that he needs it for *dawa ya wenyeji*, native medicine to ward off evil spirits. Ask a mother what she has tied around the neck of her little baby and she will tell you that it is powerful medicine to ward off the evil spirits.

It is true that education as to the true nature of disease has helped some people to drive the idea of witchcraft farther back into their consciousness, but even with these people there is an occasional surfacing of old beliefs. We find even in America, where most deep-rooted superstition has been eliminated, that hotels do not have a thirteenth floor and people knock on wood to avoid an expressed thought coming true. Do people really believe thirteen is unlucky? Well, not *really*, but then again . . . .

One of the most interesting beliefs I came across in our part of Tanzania is the fearful belief that certain men have the power to change themselves into animals, and harass other people as hyenas or lions, or sit on a rooftop disguised as a bird and listen to conversations. The most dangerous men are those who transform themselves into lion-men, thereby able to wreak revenge on their enemies by killing them. In the region around Singida, where lions are still quite numerous, the belief in lion-men is predictably strong. Many of the local people blame lion-men for most of the deaths caused by lions.

A few years ago there was a particularly striking example of this, and before it was all over, 19 people and 273 cattle had been killed by a single lion, and most of the killings went on after the local game wardens had found the trail of the lion and were trying to destroy it. The details of the story are illuminating.

South of Singida lies some of the most inaccessible bush in the world. Dense bushes grow to a height of fifteen to twenty feet, crowding one another so closely that it is absolutely impossible to penetrate into them. There are almost no trees which can restrict the ground growth, and those trees which are present are spindly thorn trees which only increase the difficulty of going through the bush. About the only thing which can move through this bush is the elephant and even he will follow ancient trails whenever he can. Tunnels lace the bush, crisscrossing through it, allowing passage of wild boar, dik-diks, leopards and lions. If a man tries to follow these paths, he is forced into a crouch or onto his hands and knees. Practically no one lives in this bush, but there are scattered areas of open land, and in these clearings one will find small villages of rather primitive people, and around the edges of this vast jungle one also will find people living.

It was in this bush that the lion-man struck, again and again and again. And it was in this bush that Chief Singi, Head Game Warden for the Singida Region, had to find the killer. His chief adversary, as it soon turned out, was not the lion itself, but Keja Makubi, an elder of a Turu clan who lived deep in the bush.

Keja Makubi was a tall, lean, very black man of about fifty. His hair was almost white, and there were small wiry white hairs sprouting from the tip of his chin. In the sunlight his chest appeared almost white also because of the heavy growth of the same kinky white hairs. His right eye was gone, lost years before when a thorn penetrated the cornea, set up an infection which eventually ruptured the eyeball and caused the entire eye to be spontaneously eviscerated. But his one remaining eye was clear and sharp, except for a small white scar just below the pupil, which had also come from a laceration of the cornea by a thorn but which had healed without loss of the eye. He dressed in a black robe, which he wore draped around his body with the end thrown up over his shoulder. The robe was his dress in the daytime and his blanket at night and it was washed once or twice a year.

Keja Makubi lived in a small house made of saplings plastered inside and out with mud. The roof was of the same construction and kept out the rains if fresh mud was constantly added to the roof after each rainy season. With him lived his wife and four sons, the elder two being married and living in separate houses in the little *boma*. None of the family had been to school, and they occupied themselves with raising cattle, sheep and goats, driving them out every morning to graze and herding them back into the *boma* every night for protection. Their religion, if you can call it that, was animistic; that is, they held in reverence a great number of gods whose homes were in the trees, rocks and rivers. Neither Christianity nor Islam had reached them, although Keja knew about both beliefs, and had early in his life rejected both, admitting that he actually knew very little about either. He was what we would call conservative, perhaps even reactionary, in that he held rigorously to the old beliefs and traditions, closing his mind to practically every new concept that attempted to permeate his tight little world of bush, clan, cattle and gods of the forest.

One of the strongest beliefs he held was that of the lion-men of Singida, so that when he heard of the rampages of old Simba, the man-killer whom Chief Singi was hunting, he was immediately on his guard. He knew who the lion really was, or thought he did, when he began to hear the reports. Of the first five people killed, four had been from a clan that lived only ten miles from Makubi's *boma,* and the fifth was of a different clan but had just recently visited with members of the clan that had been attacked by the lion, or, as Makubi would have said, by the lion-man.

The lion-man, Makubi assumed, was the old man Kelasai Okechi who lived alone even deeper in the bush than Makubi's clan. He often disappeared for days at a time. Everyone knew he was capable of all sorts of evil, and this series of killings proved that he was a lion-man when he chose to be so. And Makubi felt reasonably safe, since he had always been on good terms with Kelasai and there would be no reason for him or his family to be bewitched and attacked by the lion-man. As a matter of fact, the longer he thought about it, the more Makubi became convinced that he must, at all cost, prevent the killing of Simba, because that would certainly prove to him that he, Makubi, was truly a friend, and this would protect him and his clan from being attacked by this lion-man, or by any of his friends who roamed with him in the night.

He gathered his sons about him one night and told them what he had in mind. There was some dissension, especially on the part of the eldest, Jumanne, but he was quickly overruled by Makubi and the other sons. Their plan was to foil the capture of Simba, even if they had to spend all their time doing it. As they talked, Makubi suddenly discovered that there was a vulture perched in the tree just above their heads, and Makubi began to talk in loud terms about the plans to thwart the capture of the lion-man. Just as they broke up their meeting, the vulture rose clumsily from his perch and flew away, proving to everyone that they were indeed right in their decision.

The lion struck again that same night, only five miles from Makubi's *boma,* killing a mother and her child as they came home late in the evening with water and firewood. The child was half eaten when they were found, but the lion escaped the wrath of the people by disappearing into the bush. His tracks were clear, and the next day Chief Singi began his months-long hunt. He carried a 12-gauge shotgun loaded with buckshot, its barrel shortened to eighteen inches so that he could maneuver it quickly in the tunnels and bush-trails that he knew he would have to follow. Behind him was his second in command, Mwile Shango, who carried a .375 Magnum rifle in case the lion were seen at a distance more susceptible to rifle-fire than shotgun pellets.

Singi and Shango carried small packs on their backs with ammunition, blankets, and food so they could stay on the track for days without going back to "civilization" for supplies. They tracked the lion easily for three days, sleeping wherever they found themselves at night, usually in someone's house. Then, as they began to feel confident they would have him soon, the tracks inexplicably disappeared. They were there in the sandy soil, and suddenly they were gone. The two hunters circled the area in vain for most of the day, trying to pick up the spoor, but in the end gave up and returned to their home base at Singida.

At three different *bomas* a week later three cows were killed in a single night. Each time the noise of the cattle awoke the occupants of the houses, and they drove off the lion before he could feed. The owners welcomed the meat, feeling that it was providential that the lion had killed their cows, for now they could eat the meat without feeling guilty about killing them themselves. Some people even began calling the lion

"Kennedy" because they knew that Kennedy* had fed them before, and now was doing it again. Makubi laughed when he heard about this, because he knew that although the lion was really a man, his name was certainly not Kennedy.

But the killing of the cows put Singi and Shango back on the trail, and they followed it for over a week. Sometimes slowly, sometimes at a fast walk, they followed the pugmarks through the bush. The spoor became fresher and fresher, and soon they were crawling through a densely covered tunnel of tangled bushes, Singi in front with the shotgun, moving a few feet at a time, peering intently into the darkness of the forest around them, expecting any moment to encounter Simba. But the wind was wrong, and before they knew it, the tracks were becoming older and older, and soon they were again hours behind the lion.

They slept in the bush that night, around a fire that they alternately fed through the long night. In the morning, cold and stiff and tired from their long hours of watchfulness, they picked up the trail again and hurried on. Their knowledge of the bush was excellent, and their hopes began to rise as they saw that the lion was headed for one of the few open places in that part of the forest. Quietly they crept up to the edge of the clearing, looked out over the acre of grassland, and saw nothing except large rocks and boulders scattered over the opening in the bush. They sat for an hour, crosslegged in the shade, hoping that the lion would show himself, or perhaps was lying down somewhere in the grass where he could not be seen from their vantage point.

Finally giving up their vigil, they began to track through the grass. As before, the tracks suddenly ended, but this time it was easy to see what had hap-

* John Kennedy, then president of the U.S., whose name was known to be associated with the free food they had been given during the last famine.

pened. In the place where the footmarks ended, there was a rock, and when Singi lifted up the rock he saw the clear print of the lion underneath. They tried to guess where the next mark would be, and eventually found another one. But after almost two hours of patient turning of stones, they had advanced only about fifty feet and it was getting dark again. They tried circling the clearing to pick up the trail again, but so well had Makubi and his sons done their work that the trackers failed. They walked back through the dark to their Land-Rover and returned to Singida for the second time.

Another two weeks passed. There were a dozen more cows killed, and three more people, but in none of the areas could Singi pick up any recognizable trail. The long rains, the *masika,* began. Tracking was better when they could find the trail, but every time it rained the tracks were quickly obliterated and impossible to follow.

Singi decided they would have to wait until the lion killed again, then they would move into the area, kill a couple of cows, and bait the lion. This plan almost succeeded. They staked out a cow in a small clearing a half mile from where the lion had made a fresh kill, tied it down so that it could not be dragged off by the lion, and checked the bait every morning to see if anything had been eating it. One morning they were rewarded by actually seeing old Simba on the bait, but he heard or smelled them coming and was gone into the bush before Singi could even get his rifle to his shoulder. But they waited patiently by the bait, constructing a blind nearby, hoping that the lion would come back.

The following morning, just as it was getting light, they shook themselves awake and began their vigil again. As the dawn came across the bush, lighting up the area where the bait should have been, the two men were astounded to see that it was gone. Ropes and all.

Someone had come stealthily during the night and stolen the bait. Rage filled their hearts, but there was nothing they could do but start tracking again.

The frustrating hunt went on and on. The ingenuity of the trackers was matched time and again by either the lion or his protectors, the clan of Makubi.

But there had to come a break. It was in a sense a tragic one, but on the other hand it was ironic, for after 18 people and 273 cattle had been killed, the lion struck in Makubi's *boma* and killed the eldest son, Jumanne. Keja Makubi was confused. Why, he said, had the lion-man turned on his clan, the one clan in all the bush who had worked so hard to protect him? He called a meeting again, this time in the heart of the bush where the lion-man could not find them, and if a bird came too close, it was driven away before the conversation continued. They were taking no chances. In secret discussion, they agreed that even though the lion-man might inform on them they would never be safe until he was dead. But they must be careful. They must continue on the trail of the lion-man, staying just one step ahead of Chief Singi, and pretend to be covering the lion-man's tracks, but actually leaving them undisturbed so that they could be easily followed.

Chief Singi picked up the lion's tracks at Makubi's *boma*. Clean, firm pug-marks in the wet sand. Almost reluctantly he set out to follow them, knowing that in a day or two or three, they would disappear, having been covered with the prints of a herd of cattle purposely driven along the same route, or brushed out with branches, or covered with brush and grass, or covered with stones again. But out he went, his determination undiminished to stay with the killer until he found him and destroyed him.

Partly as cover-up for their previous vandalism, partly out of actual guilt, and partly for the thrill of revenge, Makubi and two of his sons abandoned their plans to stay a jump ahead of Singi and decided to accompany him on the trail. Makubi was a skillful tracker, better even than Singi himself, and they covered the first few miles in just two hours. Gradually the gap narrowed between the hunters and the hunted and by nightfall Makubi was able to say, with his unsurpassed knowledge of the country, that the next day they would come upon the killer, and he even predicted where the lion would be. If Chief Singi had any suspicions concerning the sudden turn of events, he was astute enough to keep such thoughts to himself. The party slept out that night, holed up in a natural *boma* of bush and thorn beside a small spring. The lion's tracks were deep and fresh where he had crouched beside the water to drink just a few hours before. The mood of the camp was exuberant. The wind was cool after a hard, hot day. The water was fresh and cold. They felt safe and secure in their enclosure of bush, and the fire flickered with a friendly glow.

They drank their thin gruel by the light and heat of the campfire early the next morning, so that by the time dawn came they were ready to follow the lion. For the last time, they hoped. And it proved to be so.

The coolness of the morning did not last long. By the time the sun was directly overhead, the heat in the bush-tunnels was stifling, airless, and enervating. Sweat dripped from their bodies and into their eyes as they pushed slowly along the floor of the forest, sometimes on hands and knees, sometimes walking in a tiring stooped position. But they were getting closer. All of a sudden they realized the lion was slowly circling a *boma,* no doubt looking it over for an attack that night. He had not eaten for three days. The *boma* appeared deserted, although lived in.

The trackers took counsel with one another. They were certain that the lion was within a few hundred yards of their position, perhaps had even seen them, and would be on the alert more than ever since he was so close to human habitation.

Mwile Shango was in favor of walking boldly into the clearing and taking up positions inside the houses to await the lion's raid that night. Chief Singi was of another opinion. He was afraid that the lion might not attack the *boma* that night, and they would therefore lose track of him again, or even if he did attack, they could easily miss him in the blackness of the night. The moon was not due up until almost 2 A.M. and would be only about one-quarter full, or slightly less. It was Makubi who suggested they continue on as they had been doing, more slowly and more carefully, since old Simba was almost certainly lying up somewhere, waiting.

The plan worked. Moving cautiously, a footstep or two at a time, Chief Singi caught sight of a slight movement in the bush across the clearing in which the houses were placed. He himself was still in the shadows of the forest, and felt quite confident that he had not been seen. Inching forward on his belly, right up to the edge of the clearing, he saw that the movement he had detected was the faint movement of the tuft of the lion's tail, as he lay in the shade of a large bush. Between Singi and Simba, however, there was a shallow but wide ravine, and it would be impossible to get closer to the lion without exposing himself. The alternative would be to circle far out into the bush and come up to the lion from the other way. Singi tested the wind. From where he was, the wind was blowing from the lion to him; if he were to circle it, the lion would pick up his scent and be gone in a flash.

He made up his mind. He handed the shotgun back to Shango and took the .375. It was not a bad shot, about 150 yards. Carefully he stretched out on the ground, took aim, and fired. There was the sharp report of the rifle, followed almost instantly by the thud of the bullet hitting flesh. They heard a bellowing roar of rage and pain, and the lion leaped to his feet and disappeared into the bush.

Singi knew that he had hit the lion, but where? Was it a mortal shot, and would they find the lion a hundred yards away, dead? Or was it a gut shot, and would they find the lion very much alive and ready to do battle with them? Not as dangerous as a leopard, the wounded lion is still a formidable adversary when wounded and cornered. The eyes of the hunting party sought each other, knowingly, for they knew what they had to do.

They crossed the clearing, past the houses, and found the blood trail. Singi took back the shotgun for he was much more likely to need it in the bush than the rifle. There was no difficulty in following the trail, and twice they could see where the lion had lain down in the grass, leaving a pool of frothy blood on the ground. Chief Singi was pleased when he saw the froth because he knew that the lion had been hit in the lungs, and would not last much longer. He ordered the party to halt, and they sat quietly for almost an hour before they started out again, a simple precaution to assure that they would find a dead lion rather than a half-dead one capable of one or two fast charges.

The lion was dead all right, and they found him, but the hunt had a less than satisfying effect on Makubi. For while they were waiting for the lion to die, he did die, and a solitary vulture found the body, and was tearing away at the soft belly when the men came upon the kill. With a squawking and beating of wings, it fought toward the sky, and to Makubi, steeped in witchcraft, it seemed to rise right out of the belly of the lion. He froze in his tracks, then started screaming at Singi to shoot the vulture. Singi, of course, refused, since scavenger birds are protected in Tanzania, and the vulture flew safely away and landed in a tree where it continued to watch them. Makubi sank to his knees, praying to whatever gods might listen, but he knew it would do no good, since Kelasai Okechi had so obviously escaped his body just in time and was now perched in the tree, biding his time, knowing now just who his enemies were, and knowing that some time in the future he would avenge himself on the man, Makubi, whom he thought had been his friend.

Simba – the lion.

4 / Baasu

There comes to each of us those disturbing periods of doubt when we wonder just why we are doing what we are, in the place where we are. It must be a universal feeling, at least among those of us who have different choices to make as we move through life. Has there ever been *anyone* who has not said to himself, at one time or many times, "Is this really worthwhile; is this *really* what I should be doing; it this really where I should be doing it?"

Did you think these questions couldn't occur to a missionary? They can. Did you think that a missionary never has to question the rightness or the wrongness, or the appropriateness, of the work he is doing? He does. He may think about it more, pray about it more, and seek guidance and counseling more, but he will still have the occasional nagging doubt about his calling. The mere fact that he feels called to a particular work in a particular place puts an onus on him that many people never have. He feels so strongly that he must not waste his precious God-given life and talents that every minute must count.

He sometimes gets to wondering if the job he is doing has to be done at all, and, if it does, does it have to be done by *him?* Maybe he should be doing something else, somewhere else. Depending on the person and on the job he is doing, these feelings may last for only a few minutes or a few days, or they may nag away at the missionary for so long that the guilt feelings about his doubts may actually affect his work and health.

In July of 1968, an incident occurred at Kiomboi Hospital that threw the whole station into an acute depression for about two weeks. I won't describe the episode, because it is over and done with, and no good would come of rehashing it. But take my word for it: it was real. There wasn't one of us who didn't wonder what this Kiomboi Hospital was all about. None of us left; I don't think any of us seriously entertained thoughts of leaving, but the wounds were deep and festering, and they healed slowly. For some, the cure was one thing, for others another. At least part of my "cure" came from the incident I am about to describe.

We had taken the weekend off to go hunting, dropping off the plateau to the west, down onto the Wembere Plains, across the new road that the Italians had built just a few years before, past the Wembere Mission Station where Pastor Elder Jackson and his family had lived for so many years, through the permanent swamp where we could see hundreds of birds in the air – sacred ibises, black and white egrets, ducks, geese, crested cranes – and then along an ancient cattle trail to the house of an old man who my friend thought could tell us where to begin hunting for eland.

The whole clan greeted us at the entrance of their *boma* and one old man strode forward to welcome us. He was, like most Wanyturu men, tall and lean and black, but the most striking thing about his appearance was the thick pair of glasses perched on his thin caucasoid nose. They looked like the typical ten-diopter lenses that we put on people who have had cataract operations, and I was intrigued. I stepped closer, and quickly saw that he had indeed had cataract surgery on his right eye. He saw my surprise, and said in nearly perfect Swahili, "I see that you have noticed my glasses and my eye. I was blind, and now I can see. I had a stone removed from my right eye at the Kiomboi Hospital. Is that where you come from?"

"Yes, sir, we do."

"Would you like to hear the story, sir?"

I glanced at my hunting companion. He nodded in agreement, so I said yes. We sat down in the shade of the nearest house, and while the women brought us millet wine and parched corn, the old man told the following story:

It all started many years ago, perhaps ten, although as you know we find it difficult to keep track of the passage of time. Each month the sun grew dimmer, and at night the light from the cookfires flickered less brightly. I refused to believe it at first; just as we ignore so many other little things in life, I ignored the fact that I wasn't always the first to see the flash of red as the impala tried to hide in the bush. I ignored, too, the fact that if I closed my left eye, I couldn't see clearly at all. I just rubbed my right eye, thinking that there must be dust in it, and when I opened both eyes I could see again.

Then one day my son and I were out on the plains together, he to tend the hundred or so cows we had, and I on my way to the next village. We had just come out from under the shade of an acacia tree where we had rested for a moment, and had stepped out onto the road again, when I felt a rough hand on my shoulder pulling me backwards so hard that I almost fell down. As I staggered backwards I heard the roar of a lorry and felt the sand from its wheels stinging my face. The wind had been blowing so hard that we hadn't heard the lorry coming. It had come from the right, and I hadn't seen it.

I knew when that happened that I was growing blind.

Relentlessly the blurring progressed. I began to use my left eye almost exclusively. I had to give up hunting, and I had once been one of the most sought-after guides in the area. For twenty years, I had received a message once or twice a month from the Bwana District Commissioner saying that he would be coming down on such and such a day and if I were free he would like to take me along as his guide. I knew where the eland were all the time, and usually I could take him to them within two or three hours. And when we got to them, always in heavy bush, he never saw them until I pointed them out to him. They stood absolutely still, their greyish-tan coats camouflaging them almost completely in the dry season bush. But I saw them. Or rather I think I saw a difference in the shadows that flickered in the trees and on the scrubby ground, and I knew that there must be something there, so I looked hard and could make out the dark shapes in the darker forest.

No longer. The District Commissioner was gone, of course, but there were still people around, missionaries and even some Africans beginning to hunt with rifles, who remembered me and asked for me when they came down. I didn't let them see how it hurt me to tell them that I wouldn't be able to go but one of my sons would be glad to go with them.

About six or seven years ago, I became completely blind in my right eye, and about five years ago I lost the remaining sight in my left eye. My first wife, who could talk to me about things like that, told me that there were bright white stones in my eyes, right in the middle where they should be black. In the bright sun of midday, you could hardly see them, she said, but at night, with just the red glow from the fires lighting our compound, they showed big as the pebbles in the river. Except once in a while, when the light struck them just right, she could see a flash of red through the white of the stones. She told me all these things and I knew I was hopelessly and permanently blind. I had, of course, seen old folks like that before, and they just sat around their houses, waiting for someone to feed them and tell them to do this and to go there. Then they died and no one really missed them because they hadn't really been there for a long time.

So I sat, too, waiting. I could tell when it was daylight and when it was dark, so I knew when to get up and when to go to bed.

One day I heard a familiar sound: a Land-Rover picking its way along the red clay path that you gentlemen followed to our *boma* from the big new road that crosses the plains. My heart beat in my chest, for I knew it was someone coming to hunt the forest that stretches out behind our houses up into the hills to the north. I wanted to leap up with joy, to shout "*Karibu*" in welcome, to slip on my sandals, pick up my spear and go hunting with the strangers.

I didn't, of course, but slouched down in the shade of the house, wondering where my grown sons were so they could greet the visitors. It wouldn't do for the womenfolk to greet anyone who owned a Land-Rover. Then I remembered that I was alone, except for my second and third wives and our young children. I called to Saidi, the oldest boy, to help me to my feet and lead me out of the *boma* to the path.

"*Hodi,*" they called and I knew from their voices that they were white men. I drew a deep breath and called out, "*Karibuni,*" and ordered Saidi to take me out to the men.

The white man is always so blunt, ignoring the common courtesies of meeting, so I wasn't surprised when one of them said right out to me in Swahili, "We're looking for a man down here called Baasu, said to be the best guide in these parts. We want to hunt eland and we're told he knows where they are."

"I am Baasu, sir. But as you can see, I am blind, and can no longer go hunting. Perhaps if you would like to wait, I can send for one of my older sons who will be glad to escape the tediousness of herding cattle and go with you."

They talked for a moment in English, and then said they would be glad to wait if it wouldn't be too long, and I sent Saidi off. The white men sat down, and I could hear one of them playing with the bolt of his rifle and it brought back a flock of memories. Then one of the men said, and I supposed him to be making conversation, "How long have you been blind, old man?"

"Two years in my right eye, and one year in my left eye," I told him.

He got up, came over to me, and I could feel him pulling my eyelids apart. His fingers were soft and smooth, and I knew he didn't work for a living.

"You know, old man, that you have a condition which can be corrected?"

I didn't know what he meant, for I had consulted with everyone in the clan who would be expected to know what could be done and they had all said, "Nothing, old man, there's nothing that can be done."

So I thought perhaps I had misunderstood the white man with the smooth fingers, since he didn't speak very good Swahili, and I asked him to repeat what he said. He said the same thing over again, this time more slowly, and added, "I do an operation in our hospital up on the plateau which is very often successful in returning sight to eyes like yours. We take the stones out of the eyes so that the light can get in again." He used the word "*mawe*"* so I knew that he understood

* "Mawe" – Swahili for stones.

what was wrong with my eyes. I remained silent, not knowing what to say next, but when they had left with my son I reflected on what had been said, scarcely daring to believe that it could be true.

Late that afternoon, I heard the Land-Rover come back, and soon the excited voices of my wives and children could be heard exclaiming over the huge eland that was lying in the back of the vehicle. For his part in the hunt, my son was given a front leg and the liver and heart and all the intestines which could be made up into good soup. I heard the doctor, for so I knew he must be, say to my son, "Tell your father to come up to the hospital some day for an examination to see if we really can do something for him."

I had the urge to call after them, "Wait, I'll come with you right now," but a decision like this was not mine alone, and would need much discussing by not only my family but the rest of the clan. I kept my silence, but later that night, as we rested after our feast of eland heart, I brought up the subject, and heard it discussed for several hours before they returned to me and said, "Would you like to go, old man?" I knew then that the decision had been made to let me go if I wanted to.

"I would like to go," I answered, and it was settled.

As I lay on the soft table waiting for the doctor to come, I could hear the voices of two young men and several girls talking quickly to one another in a dialect which I didn't understand but recognized as being that of the Iramba people who lived on the plateau. One of them pulled up my eyelid and spoke in Swahili, "His eye is ready, doctor." Then I felt a soft cloth rubbing my eye, and I could feel a burning sensation as the water ran into my eye. A hand held my head gently. "You will feel a needle, Baasu. Don't move." And there was a sharp stinging alongside my eye, and a burning ran over my eye and again under my eye. Then I felt another slight stinging right in the eye itself and a slight pressure behind it, and in a few moments all the pain was gone and I couldn't even see light. I had a momentary panic, but I could hear voices continuing in even tones, and I tried to relax. Cloths were placed over my face, then lifted slightly so that I could breathe easily.

I heard a voice just above me praying in Swahili, "God, our Father, be with this man now as we begin the operation, and guide the hands of the doctors and nurses as they prepare to attempt to return the gift of sight to this your son who is blind. God, we believe that our faith in Christ can bring to Baasu the miracle of sight, by means of the Holy Spirit working through our hands. In the name of Jesus we pray, Amen."

I could feel nothing. I could see nothing. I felt the muscles of my back and of my arms and legs relaxing. I remembered the long walk across the hot dry plains to the edge of the escarpment, my son walking ahead of me holding my walking stick behind him so that I could follow in his footsteps. Then the climb up the rocky path to the top of the plateau, then another long walk through the fields to the hospital. We had walked all day, and it was nearly dark when we arrived. We had slept in the old kitchen behind the hospital and I had presented myself to the doctor in the morning. It had not taken him long to examine me and tell me I would be admitted to the hospital that very day to have the stone taken out of my right eye later that week.

Now I was in the room where they did these things. I could hear the low voice of the doctor saying a word or two now and then, and occasionally one of the others would answer him or ask a question. There was a faint click of small instruments, and I perceived that they were actually taking the stone out of my eye, although I still couldn't see anything. Somehow the doctor had made my eye completely blind to restore its sight. In a very few minutes the doctor said to me,

"We have finished, Baasu." I could feel them sticking a cloth over my eye, and then several pairs of hands lifted me gently over onto another rolling table like the one on which I had been brought to the room. Soon I was back in my own bed on the ward, with one of the young men cautioning me not to move or sit up or roll over. Two small bags full of sand were placed on either side of my head so that I wouldn't move if I fell asleep.

As the numbness wore off I could feel a stinging in my eye, but it wasn't too much to bear and I didn't ask for any pain medicine. I lay there dreaming of the day when I would be able to see again. Although I did not then know this Jesus whom the doctor prayed to, nor did I understand what a Holy Spirit could be, I had no doubts about the success of the operation.

Several days went by, and I was allowed to move more and more and finally to sit up to eat my *uji* and *ugale*. Every few hours, the bandages were removed and some drops of medicine were put in my eye. Each time the drops were put in I could see a little bit more of the room about me, but the bandage was always put back on so that I couldn't really test my eye. But one day the doctor himself took off the bandages, held my lids open, and said, "Do you see my hand, Baasu?" I looked hard, and told him I could.

"How many fingers do you see?"

"Two," I answered. The doctor was very pleased: I could tell by his voice.

After another few days, the doctor stopped me in the hallway and asked me to come to a small room in another part of the hospital. He took the bandages from my eye, and ordered me to open both eyes. Everything was blurred, but I *could* see.

I could see the shape of the doctor and could see he was holding something in each hand. He put a pair of glasses on my nose and held a book before me.

"Can you read, old man?" he asked.

"I started to learn once," I said with embarrassment, "but I have forgotten everything."

"But you still know the letters, don't you? Try to read the letters."

I looked at the book, and there were big letters on it, and I started to read them off. The doctor and the young men with him were very excited, and told me that everything was going well. They didn't have to say that for I knew it at once when I found I could read those letters on the book. They were in English, but I recognized them because the last word was very much like our Swahili word for the same book. I read out, "T-H-E H-O-L-Y B-I-B-L-E" and I'm sure I was grinning from ear to ear. I looked around at the people watching me, and they were all grinning too. It had been a long time since I had seen faces so clearly, and then to see everyone so happy, well, it was just too much. Tears came to my eyes and I brushed them away, almost knocking the glasses to the floor.

The doctor took the glasses then and told me I couldn't use them for a while yet because he wanted me to rest my eyes for another month or so, but then I could get the glasses back. I was discharged from the hospital, and my eldest son went back to the hospital after a couple of months and got the glasses. I've used them ever since and they have changed my life.

Driving back to Kiomboi later that night, I kept seeing the face of the old man, Baasu, peering intently at me through the keyhole in his one good eye, saying, "they have changed my life." He meant that the glasses had changed his life, but he meant more than that: he meant that the doctor* and the hospital had changed his life. I got to thinking that in spite of everything, that's what this hospital at Kiomboi is all about – to change lives. I know that it changed the life of old Baasu; I know, too, that it changed mine.

* Dr. Joseph Norquist, now of St. Paul, Minn.

5/Ndurumo

We were camped out near Lake Eyasi, four hours by Land-Rover from Kiomboi. The country was flat, or nearly so, with scrubby bush and scattered acacia trees, but to the East the ground sloped gently up toward the Kindira Mountains. For the most part it was uninhabited country, although there were a few Mang'ati *bomas* on the plains, and up in the mountains lived the primitive Wakindiga people. But it was primarily country that belonged to the elephant, lion, buffalo, giraffe and antelope, and that was why we were there.

It was almost dusk on the second day of our safari. Early the previous morning Eric* and I had driven out to Chem-chem with two African friends, had hunted there one day, and then had broken camp and had gone on another two hours to our present campsite. We were sitting around the campfire enjoying some delicious impala tenderloins when we heard the rumble of an approaching car. Soon we saw a Land-

* Eric, the author's son, then thirteen.

Rover headed toward us from the direction of the lake, the dust thrown up by its wheels shimmering red-gold in the setting sun.

Two strangers climbed out of the car and approached us. They both were tall and by their speech I could tell they were Americans. The shorter of the two men was over six feet tall and looked to be about fifty-five years of age. He had a rugged appearance, angular and muscular; only a slight paunch and the earliest beginnings of a double chin gave away his age. His features were tanned and hardy, his eyes clear blue and guileless, and on his head was crammed a canvas bush hat. Around the base of the crown an irregular strip of leopard skin was held with a row of three-inch thorns – a home-made "white hunter's" hat that had cost him ten shillings and a strip of hide from his last leopard, and which to duplicate would cost some rich tourist 100 shillings at the New Stanley in Nairobi. The pockets of his khaki shirt bulged with pipes, tobacco and boxes of ammunition, and his tan shorts were held up by a wide cartridge belt filled on one side with .375 shells and on the other with .416's. I could tell that he had been around a long time. He introduced himself as Jack Shard, and his companion as John Clement.

Clement was at least 6′ 4″, his dark skin reddish-black from recent exposure to the sun, and his hair beneath the new digger hat* was long and black. He was dressed in a bush jacket and khaki shorts which looked as if they had been bought just a few days before. He was a good-looking fellow, perhaps twenty-five, and smiled easily. I took him to be a junior executive or an insurance man.

Shard came quickly to the point after we had shaken hands all around. They were in a party of four hunters, themselves and two African companions, and were still

* Digger hat – Australian army type, with one side of the wide brim fastened firmly to the crown.

at least ten miles from their camp. They said they would appreciate some water before they pushed on.

We offered to do better than that. We convinced them they should eat with us and then spend the night, and they agreed with alacrity, assuring us that their two companions would not be overly concerned about them, or at least would not bang around in the dark looking for them.

As we sat down to supper, Jack Shard explained that he had spent most of his adult life in Africa, all but the first few years as a mining engineer, and he was taking his son-in-law on this hunting safari to acquaint him with the country in which his new bride had grown up. John Clement was a lawyer from Utah, used to an outdoor life but nevertheless enthralled by East Africa.

The evening passed pleasantly, as such evenings do, with good coffee and a little conversation about the hunting (good), and the weather (dry), and it would have proceeded without the necessity for being recorded except for a chance remark made by John Clement when we had turned to the discussion of East African law and justice. He said, "I suppose that even here the long arm of the law reaches down into the bush nowadays."

"Yes, it does, John," I answered, and told him of the time the police rounded up 300 Mang'ati and held them as murder suspects for three months.

"It wasn't always that way," Jack Shard interjected when I was finished. He was sitting on the ground, his long muscular legs stretched out in front of him toward the flames of the thornbush fire, his back against the front wheel of the Land-Rover. The leopard-trimmed hat was on the ground and his balding head shone white above his tanned face. There was something about the way he said "it wasn't always that way" that stopped the conversation and made us all turn toward him. His face was frozen in hard lines and it seemed he was remembering something from a long time ago.

Then his eyes crinkled a little, the hard lines broke up, and he smiled a trifle sheepishly.

"Didn't mean it to sound so all-fired important. But I was just remembering a story I heard once about justice in the African bush."

"Tell it to us," I suggested.

"It's a rather long story," Jack Shard said.

"We're not going anywhere, Dad," John Clement said, and you could tell he hadn't been calling him "Dad" very long.

Shard pulled out a black Dutch pipe with a short curved stem and filled it slowly. I could hear a shifting of bodies as we settled ourselves more comfortably to listen.

"Well, actually, this story is about an old African man, and I heard it long ago, but the facts are true, I'll guarantee that. If you'll bear with me, I'd like to try to tell it like the old African did to a young white man:

'Ndurumo was a young man of about eighteen (the old African began) when this incident took place. It had been four years since he had spent three months in the special camp where, along with twenty other fourteen and fifteen year olds, he had learned the ways of young warriors and how they should live, and in the end had been circumcised as a sign of manhood. He now carried the long hardwood spear which had a black and silver blade on one end and a steel point on the other. He wore, as was the custom in his tribe then, a long black robe thrown loosely over his shoulders. In his ears were copper ornaments and on his fingers coiled copper rings. He stood as straight as his spear and almost as tall, and could run for hours across the plains or along the paths through the bush. Until he was circumcised he had gone out each morning with the cattle, every day for grass and on alternate days for water, but after the rites of manhood he was no longer required to do this and spent his days roaming the veld, or hunting, or making arrows with which to shoot the ostrich and the greater bustard and even kanga and kwale if he felt like crawling on his belly for an hour.

'One day was like the one preceding it and the one to follow, until he saw Laini.* That day he was hunting on the edges of the plain, where the long yellow grass merges with the thornbush, and impala and eland and wild pig come down for water. Laini was at the waterhole with half a dozen other young girls who were filling their orange-brown gourds with the murky water. Laini was of the same tribe as Ndurumo, but of a different clan, and Ndurumo had never seen her before. She knelt beside the pool, flung her headcovering over her shoulder so it would not get wet, filled the gourd and stood up, gracefully balancing the water jug on her head. As she rose, she looked directly into Ndurumo's eyes, held him there for a moment, then dropped her eyes demurely and led the other girls down the path.

'Ndurumo stood quietly and watched her lithe figure as she moved sedately, yet with captivating elegance, through the high grass. With each step her hips and long legs moved sinuously, almost voluptuously. Ingenuously, yet not completely unaware of her charm, she slowly turned her head and shoulders and glanced back at Ndurumo as he stood enchanted. The other girls watched and giggled, and with a cry Ndurumo flung his spear high in the air and raced off after it.

'Laini was about sixteen, slim and firm of body, and ready for a man. Her father was headman in their clan, tall and straight and unmatched in hunting valor, unparalleled in wit and wisdom in dealing with the various problems of his village. He knew his daughter was ready to be married, but he had already turned down

* Laini – pronounced "Lah-ee-nee."

several suitors because their fathers had not been able (or willing) to show their respect for him by giving him the 100 cows he asked. It was a reasonable request, he thought, since only if a man truly wanted his daughter, would give her a proper home, and not beat her in public, and not too hard in private, would he be willing to entreat his father to part with 100 cows. He knew that it would be the son of a headman or even a chief who would finally take Laini to his *boma,* and this was right, and the ancestors would be pleased.

'It did not surprise Laini when she saw Ndurumo at the waterhole the next evening and again the next. His appearance pleased her very much, and she knew from his bearing and his ornaments that he came from a highly placed family. As she traced the sandy path through the high grass her eyes shone with love for the young man. In the afternoon as she sat grinding corn, or making a new skirt, or as she walked the forest looking for firewood, she saw the tall, handsome warrior in her mind, and longed for him.

'Several weeks passed. Still he had not spoken to her, yet he was there at the waterhole almost every night. Then one day instead of turning away when the gourds were filled, he followed the laughing girls as they wended their way to the village almost a mile away. As the girls swung down the last little hill, Ndurumo stopped on the top of the hill where he could watch the village. He drove the steel point on the end of his spear into the ground, stood on one leg and rested the sole of the other foot on his knee. Laini could see him silhouetted against the darkening sky, motionless as the eagle on his perch. He watched until she entered her house, and when she turned to look out the doorway, he was gone.

'The next morning, two hours after the sun came up, he strode into the village and without a word to anyone walked up to Laini's house and asked her father to come out and speak with him. They talked for three hours and in the end he had made the preliminary arrangements for taking Laini in marriage. Several days later Ndurumo's father came alone to the village and after another conference with Laini's father, the final arrangements were made for the wedding which would take place in six months.

'Now the young couple were free to be together, whenever and wherever they liked, since it was the custom in their tribe to allow unchaperoned meetings between a young man and his betrothed. If she should conceive and carry his child, this was considered a certain sign that the gods favored the union. He, however, was obligated to marry her whether or not she conceived, their tribe not being so barbaric as some who require proof of fertility before a man should take a woman as his wife.

'Two months passed. Several times a week Ndurumo would meet Laini in the forest beyond the village. They would sit and talk, and make love, and roam the shaded paths together. They came to know each other, and a deep feeling grew between them. You white men do not understand our ways, and you criticize our customs, and say that we do not love our wives because we take two or three, but we believe that it is possible to love more than one woman, and when we take a woman in marriage we do not turn her out later nor do we prove unfaithful to her by going off with someone else's wife under cover of darkness. So when I say that Ndurumo loved Laini, I mean just that, and she in turn loved Ndurumo as only a woman can.

'One day they met as usual, deep in the forest, after having been unable to meet for almost three weeks because Ndurumo had been obliged to attend the death ceremonies of his father's brother. As they walked quickly to their favorite trysting place, high on the rocky crags in the hills, far away from the prying eyes of children and young boys, a leopard bounded out of a tree and disappeared down the hill into a tangle of bushes and vines. Ndurumo immediately saw the possibility of demonstrating his hunting prowess before his beloved.

'Carefully he followed the tracks in the soft sandy soil, cautioning Laini to wait for him. She sat in the shade of a giant baobab tree, watching the lithe and muscular man trailing the leopard. Soon he disappeared into the bush and she relaxed against the tree.

'The tracks were easy to follow at first, but soon the leopard knew he was being hunted, and in his cunning feline way was soon far away in the dense forest. Still Ndurumo followed, deeper and deeper into the thickets, loathe to return without the trophy he had promised Laini. After three hours he did give up the chase, having lost the track where the leopard crossed the trail of a herd of elephants and its spoor was mixed with the huge prints and was irretrievably gone.

'Ndurumo retraced his steps, rapidly now, running easily along the trails that he knew so well. When he came to the spot where he had left Laini, she was not there. He called several times, thinking she might have wandered off a bit in search of berries or water. She did not answer. Only then did he notice the imprints of sandalled feet at the base of the tree, and there in the sand was the story of what had happened. He read it as you would read a book, white man, and he started off again on the run, following the tracks of an animal more deadly than the leopard. The footprints wound around the hill, across a small plain, up another hill and then across a wide plain. As Ndurumo jogged along, he tried to estimate the possibility of returning his beloved wife (for so he considered her) to her *boma.* With a heavy heart, he conceded that the chances were slim.

'So when he caught sight of a spiral of smoke several miles in the distance, in a place where no one normally lived, he was immediately excited and more optimistic. He slowed to a walk, then stopped under a spreading acacia tree, marked the fire well, and lay down in the shade and slept.

'He awoke again as the sun was setting, and sharpened his spear on a small flat stone. A tight smile creased his face as he ran his thumb along the sharp blade. His eyes smoldered with hate and he knew the time had come to prove himself a man in the way most acceptable to his tribe. Yes, he would kill the man who had taken his wife, and he would hang his nose and ears on the rafter pole of his house so that he would always remember that night.

'The sun went down, and within about two hours an almost full moon rose in the east. Moving quietly in the darkness, feeling his way slowly through the tall grass of the plains, he had almost reached the enemy's encampment when the moon began to throw its yellow light across the veld. Stealthily now, one foot at a time, with no sound except his own breathing, he crept closer to the camp until he could see the glowing embers of the fire that had thrown up the telltale smoke several hours before.

'He knelt down on the ground and waited. An hour went by, then two, and finally he saw what he had been waiting for. A dark form rose from the ground and took several large branches which he broke up and threw on the fire. In a few moments the blaze lighted up the scene, showing Ndurumo that there were two men lying by the fire, and between the fire and the man who had just gotten up was Laini. His heart beat fiercely in his chest and his mouth was dry and hot.

'Two men. Against one. And the girl. But she would be no help. Nor did he want her help, for this he must do alone or die, or he could never again lift up his head in the pride of manhood.

'He must wait till they were asleep again. If there had been just one, his honor would have required a face-to-face meeting, but with two, anything was fair. Another hour passed. The fire flickered lower and lower. Ndurumo crept on hands and knees, feeling ahead of him to avoid breaking dried branches. Fifty yards – thirty – ten – five . . .

'He slowly rose to his full height, lifted his spear slowly and carefully into position, took two quick steps forward and drove the spear with all his power into the chest of the man closest to Laini. There was an anguished scream, which ended in a strangling gurgle as Ndurumo pulled the spear from its warm pulsating target. Laini rolled over onto her stomach and at Ndurumo's rapidly spoken order ran off into the darkness.

'The other man was on his feet, his eyes wide in terror, his hands clutching his own spear, his feet shuffling sideways in the dust, angling his body for the attack. Ndurumo circled the fire also, crouching low, the spear which he held in front of him with both hands shining a ghastly red in the eerie light. The hunted man feinted with his spear as he ducked to his right and almost succeeded in knocking the spear out of Ndurumo's hand. As he recovered, Ndurumo lunged forward and felt the steel of his spear slice through solid flesh where it held for a fraction of a second, long enough for his enemy to grasp the shaft and wrench it from Ndurumo's hands. He pulled Ndurumo's spear from his belly muscles and threw it into the darkness.

'Ndurumo felt for his knife and found to his horror that it was gone, lost in the long run he had made earlier in the day. There was but one thing to do. He must recover his spear. Dodging a thrust from his enemy he ran into the darkness, only to feel the sharp lacerating pain of a spear in his own back. Stifling a cry, he reached around and pulled the spear out of his back, and could feel the hot blood pour out of the wound and down his legs. But he was armed now and his enemy wasn't. Slowly they circled the fire again, Ndurumo waiting his chance, his enemy trying to decide whether or not to run.

'Suddenly he made his choice. He lunged toward Ndurumo, then just as quickly turned and fled as Ndurumo recoiled from the feint. Calmly Ndurumo lifted the spear to throwing position, drove the spear forward so that it whistled in the air, and watched his enemy writhing on the ground in his death throes.

'Slowly he walked over to the nearly dead man and pulled the spear out of his back. He recovered his own spear and returned to Laini who now stood mutely by the fire, feeding it with dry branches so that it glowed brightly in the darkness. He drove the tapering after-end of his spear into the ground, its bloody head vibrating before their eyes, then laid his enemies' spears in the fire where they blackened and smoked and burst into flame. He dragged the two bodies off into the bush about a hundred yards, and it was not long before the high mournful cries of the hyena ranged closer and closer and then were still.

'The blood had clotted in his wound, and in the light of the fire Laini looked at it carefully, noting that it lay beneath the last rib, just to the left side of the spine. With the primitive wisdom that you laugh at, white man, they agreed that nothing should be done to the wound, for it would heal in time if no one interfered with it.

'Their two enemies had been a long way from home, and Ndurumo knew that their clan would not find out about their deaths for several days. This should give Ndurumo and Laini time to get back to the safety of their own *bomas*. So the next morning, they washed and drank at a little pool and started off on the long walk home, across the wide plain, over the first hill, across the next small plain, and finally over the last hill to Laini's *boma,* where Ndurumo was welcomed as a warrior among warriors when Laini told the clan of his courage.

'But my story, white man, does not end here with This account of inter-tribal justice. I wish that it did, for the sake of the young Ndurumo. For in those days the tribal codes were harsh, and unrelenting, and went into action when, after several more months had passed and the time of the marriage approached, it became obvious that Laini was carrying the child of one of the dead men. There was only one thing to discuss. The child must die, that was evident, but whether or not it should be taken from the womb or be killed when it was born was the topic of long hours of controversy.

'Ndurumo wanted it taken immediately so that it would not continue to defile his wife's lovely body with its filth. Laini had no say in the matter and her wishes were never known.

'The council of elders made their decision and in the light of what actually happened their judgment was most certainly the right one. Ndurumo was inconsolable when he was informed of their irrevocable verdict: his wife was no longer his, and would not be so again until she gave birth to the baby, killed it with her own hands, and then spent six long months in total isolation from her family and friends, in a separate hut built on the edge of the circle of houses which formed her father's boma. Almost a year to wait.

'After struggling with the idea for several weeks he persuaded Laini, in direct disobedience to all they had ever learned about tribal laws, to let him try to destroy the baby and then pretend that the baby had come prematurely on its own. She protested at first, but bowing eventually to his superior intellectual strength, she submitted to his ministrations. She bled, and died there in his arms, on the great wide plains, beneath the stars and in the face of the wrath of their gods, who now would never send either one of them to the home of their ancestors.'

"As he finished his story," Jack Shard continued, "the old African stood up and moved toward the fire. The young white man, mesmerized by the eloquency of the tale, was about to ask the old man how he knew so many of the details, when the African bent over the fire to throw some sticks onto it. As he did so the folds of his robe fell away from his body and there gleaming in the red light of the flames was a thick raised scar on the old man's back, just below the last rib on the left, a few inches from the spine."

The fire had almost gone out and it was very late. I rose slowly to my feet and put some more wood on the glowing coals and sat back down again. The rest of the group was silent for a long time, no doubt thinking as I was about the withering, unsparing justice of the tribal African.

I got up again and put a pot of coffee alongside the flames to heat.

"Dad," John Clement asked softly, "there's a little more to the story, isn't there?"

Jack Shard hunched his shoulders into his worn bush jacket and a slow, sad smile played on his face.

"Just a little more, son." He paused, wondering perhaps if he should go on. "Yes," he continued finally, "the old African knew by the look on the young white man's face that he was recognized and that his name was, or had been, Ndurumo. He knew in his heart and soul that his tribal laws had never been satisfied, and he knew in his mind that the white man's laws might also claim jurisdiction over him, and he was afraid. He sat down again by the fire and spoke quietly to the young man. He asked him to retain the secret of an old man, so that he could live out his years in the peace of the forest rather than in the cold box in the white man's steel and concrete town.

"The young man agreed. Ndurumo asked him if he would pledge his silence with the blood oath of the black man's tribe. He agreed, even when he learned that the custom was to amputate the little finger of the left hand of each participant and touch the stumps together so that the blood could flow into each other's body. It was done quickly, almost painlessly, with a sharp deft blow of a broad-bladed machete, and their blood mingled there in the dark of the African night, and old Ndurumo knew his life would end outside the prison he had dreaded for years."

"Rather gruesome," I commented as I stood up and handed cups around and poured the coffee.

I only stared for a short comprehending second or two as Jack Shard reached up and took his cup with the thumb and three remaining fingers of his left hand.

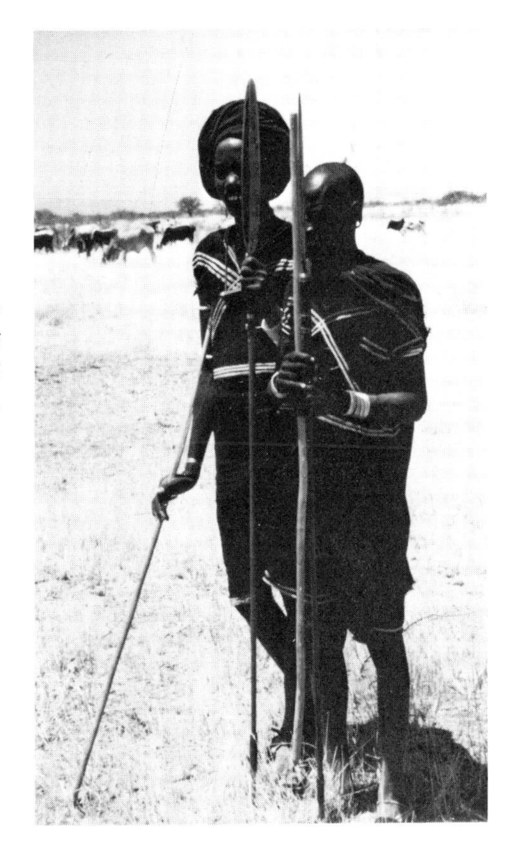

Two present-day members of the tribe of Ndurumo.

6/Yaida Chini

When we first arrived in Tanganyika in mid-1962, the role of the missionary pastor had already undergone considerable alteration. Long gone were the days when a white pastor was in charge of every congregation. In fact, there were only four churches in the Central Synod which still had white pastors.* Black pastors served all the others: Old Kiomboi, New Kiomboi, Ruruma, Kijota, Singida, Ushora, Sepuka, Iambi, and Kinampanda. In addition to this, many smaller churches scattered throughout the area had resident black evangelists and were served by the established churches.

There was an awareness among missionaries that their days were numbered in Tanganyika. Although they knew there was much left to be done (according to their views), there might not be much time left in which to do it. In 1963, a few days before he died, Rev. Doug Lundell summarized for us what he felt

* Rev. Elder Jackson at Wembere, Rev. Dean Swenson at Isanzu, Rev. Ray Cunningham at Isuna, and Rev. Orville Nyblade at Mgori.

was the task of the church in present-day Africa: 1) *creative thinking,* asking ourselves if it were possible that what was best for the local African church may not be best for the missionaries; 2) *reconstruction of relationships,* increasing the rapport with the Africans with whom we work, asking ourselves if we insist on such high standards that we destroy those relationships; 3) *reconstruction of the view of our task,* asking ourselves if we continue to find joy in our work.

During the next few years things changed even more dramatically, for when we returned in 1967 *all* of the established churches in the Central Synod had black pastors.* Three white pastors still served the Central Synod, but in roles very much the same as that of the early missionaries to Africa: the establishment of a Christian church in an area where none had yet been founded.

There was Rev. Cunningham at Gendabe, and there was Rev. Faust at Balangida, but I did not have the same first-hand view of their evangelical programs as I did with Rev. Bob Ward in Wakindigaland, so this story will concern itself with Bob and his "Digas."

In attempting to describe a surgeon, a doctor once wrote, "He must have the following attributes: the lady's hand, the lion's heart, and the eagle's eye." These qualifications may indeed be those of a surgeon, but they also describe the needs of the present-day missionary pastor in Tanzania. He must have a "gentle hand" in dealing with the Africans, he must have the "lion's heart" of faith and purpose, and he must have the "eagle's eye" to see clearly the job to be done and his part in it.

This description fits Bob Ward as the bullet fits the

* Rev. Jackson had moved to the Bible School at Ihanja, Rev. Swenson had retired from the field, Rev. Cunningham had begun a new work in an unevangelized area, and Rev. Nyblade had moved to the Theological Seminary at Makumira, near Arusha.

barrel. He is a man of action, vaccinated against hardships by repeated exposure to them. But through it all he has retained the hand and the heart and the eye of the pioneer, and I find it difficult to visualize him in any role other than as a minister to the Wakindiga.

The Wakindiga are a small tribe of about a thousand people who live in the Kindira Range along the southern shores of Lake Eyasi in north central Tanzania. Anthropologists classify them as true bushmen. Long ago the black-skinned inhabitants of the northwest corner of Africa were driven out of their homeland and migrated through East Africa into South Africa. Remnant (or relict) populations remained along the migration route, some of them to die off, others to integrate with local tribes, and still others to maintain an intact cultural group such as the Wakindiga and Sandawe and the Bushmen of the Kalahari.

They build no permanent shelters, preferring to erect little grass huts eight to nine feet in diameter on a scanty framework of thin branches. They move every few weeks or months, searching for unharvested roots, their primary diet, and they will leave areas of abundant game to find an unused area of edible roots. They also collect honey from hollows in the giant baobabs, pounding pegs into the otherwise unclimbable mammoths and scooping out the honey by the handfuls. They plant nothing, therefore raise nothing. They will move into areas of heavy berry growth during the ripening season.

The men wear a loincloth loosely wrapped around the waist, or a pair of shorts; the women wear tattered animal skins around the waist with another skin over the shoulders like a shawl for warmth when necessary. Some of the younger women are beginning to wear the cloth wrap-around *shukas* of their more advanced neighbors. Both men and women wear brightly colored bead necklaces and bracelets.

They live in single family groups, with three to seven

adults and about the same number of children, separated from their tribesmen by many miles. The reason for this is obvious: any given area can produce only so many roots, berries, and honey, and a large clan would eat itself out of a livelihood too frequently. Theirs is a continual search for food.

They are monogamous for the same reason; some cultures encourage polygamy because that means more women to till more ground and consequently produce more food, but if the food is at an unchangeable maximum already, more women only mean more mouths (and more children). There is no marriage ceremony as we know it, only a verbal contract between suitor and bride's father, and the bride-price is just a token — a couple of arrows or a skin. Although monogamous, there is a fairly prevalent custom of trading wives when both men agree to the deal.

The tribe is made up primarily of young people from fifteen to thirty. The infant mortality rate is extremely high (perhaps seventy-five per cent by the age of five), and old people are not common either. Their dead are left in the bush for the hyenas and vultures.

Their language is distinctive, called a click language, and is related to that of the Sandawe, the Bushmen of the Kalahari in Southwest Africa, and the Hottentots of South Africa. It utilizes "clicks" as we use consonants, with four different positions of the tongue against the roof of the mouth. It is a pleasant language to hear, not as musical as Kinylamba (of the Iramba tribe where we lived), but not as flat and staccato as Swahili. Most of the men also know Swahili, but there are no literate Digas, and no written Diga language.

How do you begin to work with the people under such circumstances? How do you reach them and teach them? Bob Ward knew the answer. He must go to them, live with them, learn to know them, and let them learn to know him. Is this possible with a nomadic people? How can you find them, one thousand people divided into dozens of small clans scattered across the mountains that stretch for 60 miles along Lake Eyasi and encompass an area of perhaps 1800 square miles? How can you make any permanent contacts, trusting friendships, meaningful relationships? Bob Ward considered several alternative methods for doing this, and eventually decided to live in an established community (Isanzu) on the edge of Wakindiga-land and make prolonged and frequent trips into the mountains. This he planned, and this he did. For eight years.

During the dry season he was able to make the safaris by Land-Rover even though there were no roads, and during the rainy season he went on foot, penetrating the vast bushland and mountains with his entourage of porters. Sometimes his wife, Jean, accompanied him, sometimes other missionaries. Three times I went with him. The first time, in 1962, a foot-safari, was the most memorable because I witnessed the conversion of Sha Kitundu and his ten-member clan to Christianity after many years of periodic lessons, discussions, and services by Bob Ward in the meaning of a faith in Jesus Christ. I heard him say to Bob, "*Nakubali*" (I agree), when Bob asked him if he was ready to embrace Christ as his personal Savior. Later, Kitundu was baptized Marko (Mark), and I knew him from then on by that name.

The second time, a Land-Rover safari in 1963, was the most fun because we had our wives and children with us, and we camped with a large group of Digas who were particularly friendly and allowed us to get to know them well.

The third safari, in 1967, was the toughest. It is about this safari that I would like to tell you now.

Our destination was Yaida Chini (pronounced Ee-eye-dah Chee-nee), a tiny village far up the Yaida Valley. It was sixty miles away and we would have to walk most of it. Bob had been doing this for a great many years; he was tough, muscular, hardened, and although about my age (I was forty-two then), his body was that of a fit twenty-year old. So I pared my backpack down to the absolute essentials: one change of clothing, camera, film, ammunition, rifle, water bottle, compass, one book (*Out of the Silent Planet,* C. S. Lewis), and a few toilet articles. My pack still weighed about thirty pounds, the rifle nine and a half. Bob's weighed fifty-four pounds, his rifle ten and a half.

There was a track to the first Diga village, Munguli, so we drove there in a Land-Rover packed to the ceiling with gear, with four Isanzu tribesmen jammed onto the side-seats in back. I had been in Munguli five years before, when it was the first semi-permanent village in Diga-land, with a few livable homes of grass and a few fields planted to corn and millet. There were no Christians there then, but the clan had listened long and hard to Bob Ward, and they had taken his advice in raising crops for the very first time, and he had become their friend. And they became his first Christian community in Diga-land. Sumuni, the clan leader, became Danieli, Maiombo became Daudi (David); most of the rest of that little clan also were baptized and took Christian names. Now there were permanent houses and a small church built of mudbrick, and very recently a new dispensary had been built of actual bricks and a shiny aluminum roof.

Bob hired five Wakindiga men to carry the heavy gear — tents, cots, sleeping bags, food, shortwave radio, teaching materials, etc. They were all new Christians: Filipo (Philip), Daudi (David), Marko (Mark), Musa (Moses), and Stephano (Stephen). Bob divided the gear into what he considered nine equal packs, but from the maneuvering that went on in the next few minutes it became comically apparent that some packs were more easily carried than others.

The picture I have in my mind of the beginning of that trip is strangely reminiscent of the drawings and paintings I have seen from time to time of the early explorers in Africa. There was Bob in the lead, sunburned, khaki-clad, loaded down with a heavy pack, rifle slung over his shoulder. Then Jean, unburdened except for a shotgun. Then myself, lighter pack, rifle over the shoulder, broad-brimmed hat. Finally the long, straggling line of African porters, most with their loads balanced on their heads, following the serpentine path through the bush. Children from the village ran laughing beside us, one little fellow stalking briskly at the rear of the line, matching stride for stride the ground-eating pace of the adults in front of him, then dropping off at a brush-choked ravine that seemed to mark the natural boundary of the village territory.

We walked for about four hours, stopping every hour for a ten-minute rest. Two of the stops were at waterholes deep in the forest, their edges marked with the imprints of many antelope hooves. We crossed the fresh prints of a herd of elephants and our speed increased appreciably, and then we began to climb slowly until we reached the crest of a ridge which we followed for several miles. It was as if we were in a park, the forest clear of dense undergrowth, the acacias and baobabs sharp and clean, and grass knee-high and lush.

At about three o'clock in the afternoon we reached the edge of the Yaida Valley and, since it was time for a rest-break, Bob and I threw off our packs and climbed a promontory to see where we were going. The heavily wooded slope ranged below us to the plains, then ended abruptly at the edge of the grassland. From our vantage point I could see far to the northeast and southwest, for the Valley extended as far as the eye could see. It was almost ten miles across, light greenish-yellow in color, while the ridge we were on was dark green in comparison and became a misty blue-green in the distance. I'm sure that I could have sat there forever, but Bob was anxious to get down to the Valley and set up camp before dark.

The path began to drop slowly, then more and more precipitously, and finally began to level off again. The walking became easier and easier. We were still in forest, more jungle-like than any we had yet been through, and there was elephant sign everywhere: fallen trees, huge prints in the earth made when the ground was soft and wet, and droppings as big as footballs. Wafting to us on the breeze was the unmistakable smell of zebra; a few little white birds flitted erratically about, indicating that rhinos were also nearby. We took a firm grip on our rifles.

The path leveled out, still in the forest, and we spotted a small herd of impala. Daudi and I stalked them and I shot a small one – just the right amount of meat for one meal.

We crossed the treeline, filed through dense shoulder-high grass to a small stream lined with eucalyptus trees, and pitched camp in a grove of acacia trees. We all set to work: setting up the three tents, clearing away the high grass, digging three trenches for the fires. Soon the odor of *ugale* drifted across the camp and we knew that supper was ready.

The Africans in north-central Tanzania eat twice a day. In the morning they drink *uji* (pronounced oo-jee), made by mixing a small amount of corn or millet meal in water. At night they make *ugale* (oo-golly) from corn or millet meal, adding it directly to hot water, stirring continuously with a big wooden spoon until it is a thick mass not unlike crumbly bread dough. No salt or other ingredients are added. This was what we ate that first night and almost every night. While the *ugale* was being cooked, an impala stew was simmering on a second fire, and when both were ready we seated ourselves around the third fire and ate from the two common bowls. I took a small handful of *ugale,* fashioned it into a small ball with my fingers, indented one side of it with my thumb, scooped up a bit of the stew *(mboga)* with it and popped the mass into my mouth. Except for the dryness and tastelessness of the *ugale,* it was a satisfying meal. I filled up quickly, but the Africans finished the meat, continuing to eat for another three hours until the entire impala was gone. Then they broke the bones and picked the marrow out with stiff stalks of grass. I admit I gulped just a little when I realized that some of the "meat" we had eaten were the intestines, heart, kidneys, and liver of the impala.

We were all tired and it felt good to squat with full bellies in front of the fire, the cool wind blowing through the grass across the Yaida Valley to us, carrying on it the noises of the birds and insects and frogs. In the west there was a sharply defined half-moon; the night was so dark and the air so clear that we could easily see the outline of the unlighted half also.

Kiomboi seemed far away, so much a part of an alien world that I dared not even think of places like Chicago and Eau Claire and London and Viet Nam. I wish that I really understood Einstein's theory of relativity, for if I did I might have a better insight into my thoughts that evening. For right then, camped out under that half moon, Kiomboi was far enough away that I couldn't envision anything further. And yet Kiomboi was only about forty air miles away.

So it wasn't only *miles* that separated me from Kiomboi (or London or Chicago) – it was *time.* Time, that odd E=mc squared business that few of us really comprehend. For Time seemed not only to be standing still, but I had the strange feeling that we were actually moving backward through it. Long, long ago our own ancestors must have camped in that very spot on the edge of the Yaida Valley, perhaps when the Valley was still a lake rather than a dry plain with a small swamp in the middle of it. And before that? Who knows . . . after all, only a hundred miles to the northwest was the Olduvai Gorge in the Serengeti Plains where Dr. Louis Leakey has found evidence of early man who surely must have roamed the land where we camped that night. Were these Digas who sat with us in the firelight cracking impala bones descendants of those ancient "people" just as we are? If so, they had progressed only to the level of stone-age man whereas we have reached out to the moon. In the moonlit African bush one gets to thinking all kinds of strange thoughts.

We were up at dawn. Our alarm clock was the first weak ray of cold sunlight that filtered through the acacia trees. My tent-mates, Filipo, Daudi, and Marko, rolled out of their rough grey blankets into the shivery morning air, stark naked and shining black, put on shirts, shorts, and sandals and were ready for the day. I took a little longer and the *uji* and tea were ready when I made my appearance.

The tents came down, the loads were made up, Bob led us in morning devotions, and within an hour of our awakening we were formed up into a long line, headed straight into the rising sun. Almost immediately we began to see the plains game – zebra, Tommies, wildebeeste, and a parade of ostriches which passed us going the other way, unconcerned about us, trailing a dozen young ones who were about the size of small turkeys, gray-brown like their mother.

I fell into step just behind Bob so we could talk. He showed me far in the distance, about twenty miles away, the escarpment we hoped to reach that night.

"Bob," I said after a while, "the plains are so dry I've been wondering why we couldn't have driven across."

"Could have. But then it might have rained – probably will – and we'd have had to leave the Land-Rover down here. Better to walk in and walk out than take that chance."

We talked of many things, but never about the heat and the dust and the blisters I could feel developing on my booted feet. (Bob always wore low-cut shoes without socks, and in this way kept the small irritating grass seeds from catching in the socks and causing sores.) On that second day out we talked a lot about Amos. Yes, Amos. And Daniel, and the Revelation of John. It sounded a little far-out then, even more so now, but this is what we talked about for Bob had been studying those three books of prophecy and had come to believe many things I find hard to accept.

He is convinced that the present day happenings in Israel are the last days before the anti-Christ will appear to take over the world. He will succeed not by force but by clever politics, and then the other fulfillments of prophecy will follow, including the "rapture" (the second coming of Christ), and the final judgment. Bob feels that this could be very near, even in the next ten years, and certainly in our lifetime. It is a disconcerting thought, hard to accept, and it goes against our complacency, but when I heard it from the hard, blue-eyed, sun-burned man at my side – like a prophet himself, slogging through the burning desert – I found it hard *not* to believe.

We began to pass the *bomas* of the Wamang'ati pastoral people related to the Masai, and their scattered herds of cattle and goats. We held to a thin track that angled across the veld toward the escarpment in the far distance. Stretched out parallel to the Valley on our left was the Kindira Range, in which the majority of the Wakindiga people live. It was into those mountains I had gone with Bob on the two previous safaris, but this time we were bypassing the major encampments to get directly to Yaida Chini.

Our first two rest stops were waterless and I exhausted the small supply of water I carried with me. The sun was well up, burning in a completely cloudless sky, and with the persistent wind and rapid pace we were losing great quantities of water by insensible perspiration. We left the track, headed back into a small patch of trees, and there found a tiny pool with green scum floating on top. It looked like a fine mountain spring to me and I scooped up a canteen-cup full and drank voraciously. I passed the cup around and by the time all had had their fill, the water hole was nearly dry. The salty peanuts we had for lunch made me more thirsty, but I knew that we needed the salt almost as much as the water.

There was no shade on the track as we pushed on. The tallest vegetation were scattered thorn bushes scarcely two feet high, but several miles in the distance was a tall tree which looked like an oasis in the Sahara. My pack was getting heavy, my feet blistered, and I had given up my rifle to Daudi who carried it along with his heavy pack. When we reached that tree across the endless plains we threw down our packs in relief and lolled in the tall green grass. No sooner had I flattened out than I heard the startled cry, "*Siafu!*" and soon everyone was up on his feet, shouldering his pack or throwing it up on his head again. Red ants! Thousands of them, crawling up our hands and our pants' legs, biting viciously with a sting like a scorpion. We spent the next fifteen minutes picking ants out of our clothing and off each other's necks. Let me tell you that was a wild time.

Two hours later, with the sun now in the two o'clock position, we reached a slight rise with a few large clumps of bushes on top. I struggled up the incline, nearing the point of exhaustion, and literally fell into the shade of a bush. I was about to lose face, but you know at that point I couldn't have cared less, so when Daudi took my pack and divided up its contents among the other porters, I was thankful to him for having sensed my discomfiture. "Thanks," I said, but was completely ignored. He merely pointed to a row of trees across the dry, parched plain.

"There will be water there," he said. Without the pack I thought I could make it, although it was about four miles away. I silently chastised myself for making such a safari without adequate conditioning, but it was no good thinking about that then.

We took a long rest, almost a half hour, then started out again. I felt light as a feather, gun-less and pack-less, and for the better part of an hour I strode along with the rest. At the end of the hour, we sank down to the ground for a rest, and when we got up again I was stiff and weak and knew I was done. Gradually I dropped farther and farther behind, until Daudi, who was next to last in line, was almost fifty yards ahead. He kept turning around to see if I were coming, knowing that we had to push on because if we stopped there we had neither shade nor water.

My legs were giving way, and finally would go no more. I lay down on my side in the dust, my head swimming and my breath coming in labored gasps. My hands were numb, and as I watched them they began to contract so that the thumbs were pulled against the palms and the hands pulled down toward the wrists. Sweat poured across my forehead, running down the frames of my sunglasses, and I remember thinking with relief that I could still sweat. Daudi and Marko came back anxiously, and half-led, half-carried me to one of the tiny thorn bushes where I could at least get my head in a small patch of shade. Jean came back and soon the entire line had stopped to watch. Bob came back and told me they would go on to get water and send someone back with it. I nodded dumbly.

Jean and Daudi stayed with me while the rest of the line swung off through the blaze. I could feel my fingers starting to relax, and in an hour Filipo came back with a full canteen of cool water. It was the color of water that has come out of a tap unused for several years, but I gulped it thankfully. Where the water spilled out onto the sides of the canteen it dried a bright red mud. Jean poured a packet of Tang into the canteen and that helped some. But I could feel, literally *feel*, the strength moving back into my arms and legs as the water was sucked out of my stomach into the tissues. I drank that entire canteen full of Tanged-up muddy water and walked the remaining two miles to the water hole. My tent was up, the Africans were seated around the fire preparing supper, and I crawled onto my cot and dropped off to sleep, my last thoughts being the long miles of open grasslands, the increasingly large numbers of animals scattered across the plains, the Mang'ati *bomas* and the big red mudhole from which I had been drinking. We had walked twenty-two miles.

I awoke about two hours later, much refreshed, and realized that I had heard a shot. I pulled on my boots, zipped up the mosquito lining on the tent, and stepped outside. Bob had shot a Tommy for supper, and the men were carrying it in to get it ready for the pot. I wasn't the least bit hungry. Jean had made some coffee, and with a goodly dose of powdered cream and sugar it almost tasted like coffee. And it was wet. I drank three or four big cups before my thirst began to leave.

The next morning we were off again, and with only about five miles to go I felt capable of taking back my pack and rifle. We reached Yaida Chini about noon, after a stop at a lonely game ranger's camp, and spent a couple of hours setting up camp under a giant wild fig tree alongside a stream. Curious Digas came to watch us and to sit on their haunches talking to us as we worked. I found that these people at Yaida Chini were not there of their own free will. They had been rounded up in the hills by the government and forced to settle in that place, a part of the growing scheme to push and pull the Wakindiga people out of their primitive, nomadic ways. They were supposed to be the first *Ujamaa* village in Diga-land. Actually they were miles from their homegrounds, and although their houses were better and their crops were growing, they were not happy. Indeed, shortly after our visit there they vanished from the place, scattering to the mountains where they felt they belonged.

I could not help contrasting this encampment with Munguli, where we had left the Land-Rover, and where the people were living in what might be called an *Ujamaa* village, but of their own accord, bonded together by a common goal and a common religion and a common desire to improve their lot. Here in Yaida Chini they were forced to live together, forced to plant corn, forced to build mud-brick houses, and checked on periodically by an officer of the government who instructed them in what was expected of them and taxed them when they began to show signs of bettering themselves.

There is no place in the world where you can force people to live differently from their accustomed routine and expect them to like it, even if you can prove statistically and scientifically that they are "better off." What good is a house, what good is a cornfield, what good is an ordered society, if the people do not feel free to live according to their own ideas, at least if those ideas do not conflict with the laws of the country or with the freedom of others to live as *they* please?

In Munguli the people came of their own free will, they saw the houses and the cornfields, and they saw what there was to see and if they liked what they saw, they stayed. If they liked their own life better, they left, and no one chased them down and made them come back. Because a man is primitive, because he is uneducated, because *you* can't understand why he lives the way he does – this is no reason to say to him, "You will live in Yaida Chini, or Munguli, or Dongabesh, or Endasiku, or we will hunt you down and make you come back."

We stayed just three days at Yaida Chini. I won't detail the days for you, but there were some events that should be recorded. Bob didn't spend all day, every day, teaching and preaching, but he did hold a *mafundisho* (teaching session) every evening, and there was a daily song-and-worship service. The rest of the time we just lived there. Bob spent a lot of time reading, leaning back against the giant bole of the fig tree by our tent. Jean busied herself about camp. I loafed and read. I finished *Out of the Silent Planet* and started on *A High Wind in Jamaica* (Richard Hughes), read the latest *Time* magazine word for word, and also a fascinating report on the Sonjo Tribe in northwest Tanzania.

Each afternoon we went swimming in a deep cold hole a hundred yards from our camp. The Digas' children swam every day, too, playing water games just like kids everywhere – diving, splashing, ducking, paddling, breath-holding, laughing, even singing hymns at the top of their voices while doing a little dance in the water. I rather think the latter was done for our benefit for we loved to sit on the bank and watch them.

When the small fry were done, the older girls went in shyly, taking off their clothes only after they were deep in the turbid water. Like their elders, they were not shy about uncovering their breasts, and I asked Bob about this. He said that he had also wondered about this, so he once had asked an African pastor about the breasts as sex symbols in the African culture. The pastor said that despite the semi-nudity of many African tribeswomen, the breasts do definitely have sexual significance to the African male, but the buttocks much more so. This was interesting to me because I had so often heard that the attempt by early missionaries to cover up the women was contrary to their culture since the breasts were *not* sexually significant.

I saw several patients during the three days we were there. Perhaps the most pitiful one was a very young girl who was seven months pregnant and had been placed outside her grass hut in the sun because she had gone into labor prematurely. I talked to her and examined her, and she had indeed begun to have strong uterine contractions. But she also had malaria; I was convinced of this, even without a blood slide. And I knew that malaria could precipitate early labor. I started her on very high doses of chloroquin diphosphate, and within hours she was improved and her labor contractions had begun to abate. The next morning she was up and about and it was with some difficulty that I convinced her she should continue to take the medicine. I don't know what eventually happened to her, but she was fine when we left the camp several days later.

One evening just at dusk Bob called the clan together for *mafundisho*. The sun was low on the horizon. Black clouds and thunderheads were gathering over the escarpment and streaks of rain were already rolling out over the dry plains we had just crossed. The people gathered slowly, about fifty altogether, twenty of them men, and sat under the giant tree just at the edge of their village. Jean led us in the most popular hymn that we sang in Africa, "*Mungu ni Pendo*" (God is Love), and then "*Jesu ni Rafiki Yetu*" (Jesus is our friend, or What a Friend We Have in Jesus).

Bob then talked to the group, using large charts which he hung from a branch of the tree. He said that God is all-seeing, He sees you, He sees me. Satan is also omnipresent, in everything, in everyone, even in the animals which all have their faults. There was a picture of a peacock strutting, a dog in his own dirt, a hidden snake waiting to bite, a leopard lurking in the forest, and a turtle from which native medicines are made. Bob made the point again that God is Love, and can help man to overcome his own faults if He is trusted. He explained that God first loved us, and trusted us, and His love and trust are always there, embodied in Jesus Christ, who was sent by God to show us God's love.

We went back to the tent and turned on the shortwave radio. Oh, it was good to hear news from home: flamethrowers and tanks were massing at the DMZ in northwest South Viet Nam; Wilson was in Washington to try to bolster his sagging image; 98 people were down with a plane over the Himalayas and 27 people went down with a plane in the Amazon Valley.

Since we were planning to start our walk back to Isanzu on Sunday morning, Bob held a service on Saturday morning and preached a short sermon with the aid of several charts. I think it might be interesting for the reader to hear the last sermon Bob Ward preached to the Digas in Yaida Chini before they escaped the village and returned to the bush. Remember Bob had been teaching and preaching in Diga-land for more than eight years and many of his listeners had a clearer view of the religion we call Christianity than many of the readers of these words. Remember, too, that these people were students of the raw, basic life that you and I have not only forgotten but never really knew. They had a deep understanding of the instincts which govern man's existence in a place where it is death to fail to understand.

Bob Ward preached in Swahili. Every sentence was quickly translated by Daudi into Kikindiga, the tribal language, so that the women and children could understand. The intervals of translation gave me a chance to take down the sermon almost word for word:

"God is the ruler of our world just as Julius Nyerere is the headman of Tanzania. But Mr. Nyerere is just the head man in *this* country. God is the king over all. He is holy, and when we reach eternity we shall see Him face to face, eye to eye. God has unending strength – strength to do everything. He knows all; He even knows the Wakindiga are held in Yaidi Chini, and if they fight, He *knows*.

"God *is* the ruler. His voice is heard in the Bible and in the voices of His servants. You have heard His Word from evangelists, from pictures, and in many other ways. You have learned how to follow God. For in this world there is pain, long trips, thorns, hard farming — great trouble is truly here, and it comes from Satan. But Satan was cast out by God into a sea of fire so that there will be a new world when the old world passes away. As the young man becomes old, as the grass withers and dies, so will the world grow old and pass away.

"If you choose God, Satan is cast out. If you choose Satan, you choose darkness.

"The servant was sent. That servant is the Word of God — the Bible — to drive out the bad things from man's heart. Like a doctor's needle that hurts a little in order to heal, the Word of God hurts a little and causes some trouble before Satan is driven out — because we *like* the sins of our heart.

"When man finally receives God, he receives peace in his heart. All enemies are driven out but don't forget that they remain nearby — if they have the littlest opening, they try to get back in. As we eat every morning and evening, so it is necessary to take in God's Word every day — to 'be fed' each day.

"Here you see a picture of Jesus on the cross. He came to earth as God's Son, to live like other people, to give His blood, to save us from our sins — to cleanse us — to open our eyes. The trouble is that we can choose to keep our eyes closed. But remember that day by day, minute by minute, man is able to keep all these things in his heart and to destroy the enemies in his heart, for nothing gives happiness to man like the love of God in his heart — not cows, money, or anything else.

"Some men have just one eye closed. They sin just a little, and then their enemies begin to return into their hearts. But the cross of Jesus can drive them out. You lie if you think that being baptized or going to church every Sunday makes you a Christian — if you think that, you are making yourself No. 1, and Jesus No. 2.

And when you reach the end of life, Satan will be standing there in the middle of your heart and Jesus will be standing outside watching sadly. But if you have Jesus in the middle of your heart, and remember that God is with you, then you will receive peace when you leave this life."

As Bob sat down and Jean got up to lead the "congregation" in a closing hymn, I wondered how many of those people had understood what he was saying. I looked around at the intent faces of the men close to me – Daudi, Marko, Stephano, and a few of the men from the local village, and I no longer wondered – I knew. They understood.

We broke camp late that afternoon and walked the few miles to the Ranger's camp. He wasn't there, but we cooked our *ugale* in the old fireplace in the hollow of the ancient fig tree overlooking the river, looked for *kwale* in the brush, sat around the fire in the evening and talked about all those things one talks about around a fire in the African bush, and went to bed early.

We were up at five the next morning, sipped our *uji* and coffee in the pre-dawn chill, and as the sun came up along the Ranger's airstrip we were off for home. My pack was down to about 15 pounds, Daudi was cheerfully shouldering my rifle, and Marko had my camera draped around his neck. We walked straight down the Valley of Yaida, the sun climbing higher and higher until it began to turn toward the west. There was water this time, left by the rainstorm we had seen over the Plains a couple of nights before. I tried to find the tiny thorn bush that had shaded my head four days before, but it had melted into the expanse like my remembrances of that ordeal. We saw zebra and Tommies and wildebeest and hartebeest standing in watery mirages in the shimmering heat. Two small hills on the left of the valley moved by us with agonizing slowness as the long miles crept past. A completely naked man stopped to talk to us and stood aside to let us use the thin worn trail through the grass. We did not make the mistake again of resting in the shade of the one tree in that vast wilderness.

Clouds began to form up in the west, blotting out the sun and much of the heat, and just as we pitched the tents in the acacia trees at the far end of the valley the rain came in torrents to cool us. Daudi and I took a shotgun and pushed through the dripping shoulder-high grass alongside the stream and got two *kwale* for the *ugale* stew. We mixed them in with a few pieces of leftover wildebeest, heated up a packet of tomato soup, and ate our last supper of the safari. A lion roared throughout the night, and a hyena prowled close by the tent, its cadenced call sounding across the veld.

It was a short four-hour walk back to our Land-Rover at Munguli the next morning. We stopped three times: once for Clementi to repair the straps on his sandals, once to change our bullets to hard points when we suddenly came across fresh buffalo tracks and elephant droppings, and once for water high on the ridge only an hour from Munguli.

I have written this as if it were all something that

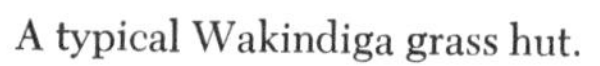
A typical Wakindiga grass hut.

happened in the past, and in fact it did, I suppose, but it didn't just happen once and then disappear into thin air. The Yaida Valley is still there. The Wakindiga are still there – Danieli, Marko, Stephano, Daudi, Filipo, the malarial woman who was pregnant, the kids in the swimming hole, the inhabitants of Munguli, the whole tribe of Digas scattered across the endless mountains. Bob Ward's life and words are still there, although he has moved from Diga-land to a different town and to a different work. His words were The Word, and his life was The Word, and he left behind him a book that contains all that man needs to know about the Word. His rough, calloused hands were the "lady's hands" that dealt firmly but gently with the lives of the most primitive people on earth; his heart was the "lion's heart" that kept his mind and body and spirit aflame with the message he was called upon to take to the Kindira Mountains; his eye was the "eagle's eye" that quickly and eagerly took in the task which needed to be done. So Bob Ward, missionary pastor, is still there, too, his thoughts and words and deeds inextricably interwoven into the fabric of life of hundreds of God's children who might never see him again.

Baobab tree.

7/Mduguyu

"It may be said that hunting is ever a love-affair. The hunter is in love with the game, real hunters are true animal-lovers. But during the hours of the hunt itself he is more than that, he is infatuated with the head of game which he follows and means to make his own; nothing much besides it exists to him in the world."

So wrote Isak Dinesen in *Shadows on the Grass.* There is a heady fascination about hunting, especially in Africa, and this excitation is bruited about the world, galvanizing men and women to go to Africa "on safari." The word safari was born in Africa, derived from the Arabic* word *safar* which means simply "a journey." There is a magic in the word for most Americans because it does not merely connote a trip to the nearest store for groceries, although this *is* a safari, but rather conjures up the classic images of hunting safaris in the bush of such countries as Tanzania, Kenya, or Mozambique.

* Approximately one-third of Swahili words come directly from the Arabic, the other two-thirds being Bantu in origin.

I suspect that few aspects of life in East Africa have been more inaccurately represented than the big-game hunting. There are, of course, good reasons for this. The average sportsman reading his magazine for vicarious thrills reads almost entirely about the expensive hunting safaris sponsored by professional hunters ("white hunters"), and on these hunts it is common for the client to kill elephant, lion, leopard, Cape buffalo, and rhino, as well as zebra, pig, kudu, and one or two of each of the many species of antelope — eland, gazelle, wildebeest, hartebeest, roan, sable, oribi, impala, and so forth. These are highly organized hunts with men who know the country and know how to get the game, and who are aided by a veritable army of trackers, spotters, skinners, cooks, sweepers, tent-men, launderers, waiters, drivers, mechanics, and personal servants. The client lives very much as he does at home, perhaps in more ease, except on the road when he must take the bumps and dust whether he likes it or not! He does not become involved in finding the game, cleaning it, butchering it, or in handling the trophies. He need not worry about car breakdown, water, food, or where his next drink is coming from.

I never have been on a hunting safari with a professional hunter, nor will I ever do so. I never have had the necessary thousands of dollars to spend in that way. There is too much senseless killing for the sake of killing, with dead game left to rot while the white hunter and his party return to their martinis. There is too little real "hunting" on the part of the client, who all too often is taken by Land-Rover to an elephant or a rhino or a lion which has been followed for days on foot by the real hunters (the local African trackers), and then gets out of the car, shoots the animal, and has his picture taken with "his" trophy. In fairness I must say that this is not true of all professional hunts, nor of all visiting hunters, but it is true of enough of them to give the entire scheme a bad name in Africa.

I love to hunt. I hunted in Africa whenever I had the chance (once or twice a month), but we found our own game, stalked it carefully so that we got good clean kills whenever possible, and utilized all parts of every animal for some purpose. The one exception was a lion I shot with Ramadhani Kamata and which I detail in Chapter 11. I still get sick every time I think about it. We rarely left a wounded animal in the bush, and then only after an exhaustive search had been made.

Besides enjoying the hunt, I went out for a number of other reasons. Wild game was our only source of good meat. Hunting was really our only recreation, since there was no TV, movies, plays, concerts, or social gatherings except our own station picnics at the time of the full moon. And hunting got us out into the bush where we could live with and talk to the local people. This book would have remained unwritten without the stories and information I garnered on our safaris. I really felt I got to know the people with whom we lived and hunted.

So, on my weekends "off call," we packed up the Land-Rover and went off into the bush, sometimes just a few miles, sometimes farther. There were two areas just off our plateau, Mduguyu and Chem-chem, which were nearly devoid of human habitation, and here there were large concentrations and great variety of game. During my first tour in Tanzania ('62-'63) we usually hunted in Chem-chem, but in '67-'68 we were cut off from that fascinating area most of the time by road washouts and therefore it was closer to Mduguyu.

I hope non-hunters will not skip quickly through this chapter, thinking it is entirely devoted to the hunt. It is a hunting story, true, but it is more than that: it is a vehicle to get across some other ideas that I think important.

It was winter, July, with the Big Dipper upside

down in the north (pointing to an invisible Polaris), and the Southern Cross high and bright in the south. The Milky Way lit up the landscape white as snow, and the nighttime temperatures were well down into the '50s. The summer floods which had paralyzed transportation for months had dried up, leaving the plains sere and cracked. The rivers were nearly empty and we knew we could go anywhere we wanted to with the four-wheel drive Land-Rover. Up until Friday we didn't really know where we might go, but that evening the decision was made for us.

Eric and I were sitting in the living room, watching Barbara's* rabbit trying to drink out of a coke bottle, when a familiar green Land-Rover pickup truck ground to a halt in the sand driveway in front of the house. I got up to welcome Nosoro Seif. Nosoro was a half-African, half-Arab friend of mine who was chief mechanic at the Government offices four miles from the hospital. Originally he came from Mafia, a tiny island off the coast of Tanzania, an island with a local (and I think international) reputation for excellent big-game fishing. He had spent fourteen years with the German Army, and had lived in Germany for several years during the Second World War.

Nosoro spoke English, German, Swahili, and Arabic, all fluently, but in my house he spoke in English, interlarded with Swahili words which did not translate easily. Except when working or hunting, he wore the floor-length white robe and small white skull-cap of a Muslim. I knew that he was a devout practitioner of his religion, for I had been hunting with him many times during the months of Ramadhan and even on the hottest of days he took nothing into his mouth from dawn to dusk, and with never a word about it. He never ate pork, not even the wild boars we shot out

* Barbara – the author's daughter, then eleven.

on the plains, and of course never ate any meat unless it had been ritually killed.

I suspected he had come this evening to invite himself on our weekend hunting trip. I always welcomed him, and really meant it, too, for I liked to have him come along. He knew the country, he knew the local people so we could always count on good guides, and he knew everything there was to know about motor vehicles so if there was any way to get a crippled Land-Rover home he would get it there. And besides, he was good company. He wasn't a smiling man, nor a joker. In fact, he was usually of stern countenance, without a real sense of humor, but he was kind and sensitive, and always seemed to me to be interested in other people's welfare rather than his own. When we were together, hunting or elsewhere, he usually made the decisions because he was that kind of a man, but it was amazing how often those decisions reflected what he knew I wanted to do rather than what I knew he wanted to do.

He eased his short stout body onto the edge of one of our *meninga* wood chairs. He seldom sat back in the chair, seldom seemed completely at ease in my home, although he would come often and talk with me for an hour or more. Even after almost three years of frequent meetings and hunting trips, I was still "the Doctor," and never once did he call me by my first name, although he was older than I by about ten years.

In good African fashion we talked aimlessly for five or ten minutes. I knew why he had come, although just how he knew I was going hunting I don't know! There was no "jungle telegraph" that I knew anything about, but it was truly fantastic how everyone in the whole area seemed to know almost before we did what we were going to do.

"Nosoro," I said, "we're going hunting tomorrow, but I can't make up my mind where to go. Got any ideas?"

"Mduguyu, Doctor, just past Nlandala. Big elands

there. Very big. Also very big lions. You have a lion license, *sivyo?*"*

"Yes, I've got a lion license. Are there more lions there than out past Chem-chem in the Eyasi area?"

"Many more, Doctor, many lions there. They come right into your camp. You must drive them away with the Land-Rover."

I wasn't sure how badly I wanted to do that. "Don't you even have to bait them, with a zebra or a wildebeeste or something?"

"We would bite them, yes, Doctor, but it is not necessary always to put out a bite. One time they came right into our camp and we had to drive them out with a Land-Rover."

Perhaps you noticed that all of a sudden it was "we" who were going hunting. I smiled to myself, and shot a look at Eric. He also was trying to hide a grin. But he liked Nosoro, even though when he was along Eric usually had to ride in back.

We talked some more, and made plans to leave the following morning about ten. Nosoro would be taking one of his men with him, and I would be taking Eric and Godson Makala, our young gardener, making a party of five. We would pick up two or three more local Africans at Mduguyu. It was imperative that I know how many people would be going, because the Africans never took any food or water. I had found that out the hard way on my first hunting trip years before! Africans expect to camp by a water-hole or a stream, and they expect to have meat in camp the first night. Usually both these requisites held, but if they didn't, I was expected to have both food and water in the Land-Rover and I always did, after that first time.

When Nosoro had gone, Eric and I walked down to Eliasafi's house to check on our Land-Rover. It was considered to be in good condition; Eliasafi had welded

* Is it not so?

a crack in the frame just above the front axle, had repaired a leaky radiator, and had replaced the left rear shackle bolt. I had had to put in a small shackle bolt a couple of weeks before because I was 200 miles from home and the bolts I had with me were all the wrong size. It had held up all right, partly because we'd had to travel fifteen to twenty miles an hour to stay back with Rev. Jackson's party: he had a broken mainspring and couldn't go any faster.

The next morning we assembled our gear on the sand in front of our house, and began packing it into and on top of the Land-Rover. We weren't equipped quite like Professional White Hunters but we were prepared for almost every eventuality: tent, sleeping bags, blankets, camp-cots, flashlights, gas-light, tarpaulin, one five gallon jerrican of boiled water for drinking, two jerricans of unboiled water for all other purposes, three jerricans of gasoline, an old mosquito lining from a discarded tent, canvas camp chairs, two old card tables, knapsack with twenty pounds of salt, box of ammunition, two boxes of food and utensils, shovel, machete, four guns (30-06, 30-30, .22, .410), an old suitcase with changes of clothing, cameras, binoculars. We had a spare wheel on the hood, and another one lashed on top. In the tool box under the front seat were wrenches, pliers, hammer, hot-patches, fan belt, shackle bolts, friction tape. In the compartment behind the front seat were two jacks, crank, plastic water jug, motor oil, cleaning rags, and tire irons.

Most of the lighter gear was lashed under a tarp on top of the car, and the heavier gear was packed into the back half of the car, prevented from moving forward by planks set crossways in the middle of the carrying compartment. With Godson Makala and Eric in back, I drove down the sand lane from our house to the main crossroads of the mission station, turned right past the water tower (an ungainly rectangular structure which was filled by pumps located about a mile behind the hospital, and which then fed the mission by gravity-flow), and on through the village of Kiomboi. We skirted the edge of the main square, and could see that it was, as usual, filled with people, vendors of fruits and vegetables, children playing in the dirt, dogs, goats, a few clots of young men in Western dress with nothing to do except hope that next week there would be some work for them.

We swung west for four miles to the *boma* to get Nosoro Seif, stopped to pick up two nurses who were walking there to see friends, and arrived at Nosoro's house at about ten o'clock. I wasn't surprised when his wife and children informed me that he was over at the garage. We drove the half mile slowly, occasionally waving at people we knew, happy to be away from the hospital, and not really in a hurry to get anywhere. Or should I say *I* wasn't in a hurry? Eric was impatient to get to the campsite, and anxious to zero in his 30-30, which had just come from the States the week before. I didn't blame him. The gun was a pretty little thing, a Model 94 Winchester, the "gun that won the West." It was more than adequate for the plains game if someone else with a bigger gun were along to back it up in case some dangerous game showed itself.

The most popular gun in Tanzania is the .375 caliber rifle. Some people, of course, will have several high-powered rifles, but most of the men I knew were missionaries and had to settle for just one, and that was usually the .375. It's a lot of gun for small gazelles but not *too* much, and it's a lot of security with its high velocity and high "knock-down" power.* A somewhat less common though still widely used rifle is the 30-06, a 30 caliber rifle first put into production in 1906. It is

* With a 300 grain silver-tip magnum cartridge, the muzzle-velocity is about 2500 feet per second, and decreases very slowly: 2300 at 100 yards, 2000 at 200 yards. The energy generated in foot-pounds is about 4300 at the muzzle, 3400 at 100 yards, and 2700 at 200 yards.

a direct descendant of the famous 30-03, the Springfield rifle, and is an excellent all-around gun, especially for the man who has only one high-powered weapon.* Eric's rifle, the 30 caliber Winchester, is an easily handled, light-weight gun, an excellent model for a boy to begin using, although it won't stop a buffalo or a rhino.**

We found Nosoro, gave him a ride home, and within a few moments were on our way, back through the village, south through dense green forest along the now-dusty road, past the abandoned gold mine and Don Mustard's old house in the shadows of the giant fig tree, across the Kirondatal River to the junction with the East-West Road that ran erratically and bumpily for 765 miles between Dar es Salaam and Mwanza. A few miles on the smoother gravel, and we turned off to the south again just above Ulemo. Eric yelled "Watch out, Dad," too late for me to slow down and soften the jolt as we hit a drainage-trench cut across the road. I drove slowly for a few hundred yards while we waited for something to fall off or fall apart. Nothing drastic happened, but I was afraid to get out and look at the newly welded crack in the frame.

For the first ten miles, almost to Ndago, the road was no worse than our road into Kiomboi, but past Ndago it became progressively narrower, bumpier, more rutted, and finally was little more than a two-wheel track. Just past Ushora we began to drift downward just a little and could see the Plains of Wembere way off in the distance. For ten miles or so we traveled along a ridgeline, with small farms on either side of the

* With a soft-point 220 grain cartridge the velocity at the muzzle is 2400 feet per second, at 100 yards 2100, at 200 yards 1900. The energy at the muzzle is 2900 foot-pounds, at 100 yards 2200, at 200 yards 1700.

** With a 170 grain cartridge the velocity at the muzzle is 2200 feet per second, at 100 yards 1900, at 200 yards 1600. The energy released is 1850 foot pounds at the muzzle, 1350 at 100 yards, and 1000 at 200 yards.

road, but with uninhabited bush beyond. Some of the hills in the near-distance were laced with the tracks and broken-tree meals of elephants, and I remembered with a pang of nostalgia an eland hunt down there with Fred Malloy five years before.

The edge of the plateau is at Urugu, but one does not drop off suddenly at this point as he does if he goes north, west, or east. Rather, the descent is gradual, the two lanes of sand winding through the dense bush for almost ten miles before the road levels off and one finds himself on the Plains of Wembere. Near the bottom of the hill we stopped to pick up Ramadhani Kamata, and twenty to twenty-five people came out to greet us. Nosoro and Ramadhani were soon laughing about the time they had been elephant hunting and were charged by a big bull. Apparently Noroso had stood his ground, firing pointblank, and had run out of shells for his .458. When he reached back for his .375 from Ramadhani he found the gun lying on the ground and his faithful gunbearer a hundred yards away, putting as much distance as he could between himself and the behemoth. I marveled that the two men were still friends, and that they could laugh at such danger.

Eric was thirteen then, tall and slim and straight, and I caught several of the younger girls eyeing him intently. He seemed unaware, however, and I never said anything to him about it. He looked the part of a hunter all right, in once-dark, now-faded blue jeans, tan hunting shirt, my old Marine fatigue jacket (only a little too big), scuffed safari boots, knife at his belt, tossing a 30-30 shell up in the air. Only his boyish face with a few pimples gave him away, and when he spoke it was sometimes in the deep bass of manhood and sometimes in the high-pitched voice of childhood.

Where else, except in the bush of Africa, or in some very similar place, can a father so readily watch the emergence of the man his son will someday be? Where else can he witness the testing the boy undergoes, the hot sun and other hardships, the interplay of emotions when confronted with a new set of values, the give-and-take between the boy and other men (both blacks and whites), the stench of failure and the scent of success? Under what other circumstances can a father so readily nudge the boy with a word, show him with a deed, mold him into the kind of a man he wants him to be? In the hurly-burly world of modern America, life is too fast and seemingly too short, the opportunities too infrequent, the directives too much without solidarity, and father and son grow up together yet too far apart.

Ramadhani and a friend of his came with us and we started off again on the track to Mduguyu, the *gundi* village, where the seasonal work of collecting gum-arabic was in full swing. In the village we slowed down to say a few words of greeting to friends, and continued on toward the old baobab tree where we knew we would find water and shade. It was high noon, the sun burning away all vestiges of the cold night past, and we knew the game would be sheltered under the trees for several more hours. But there was one lone impala standing 150 yards from the track and Eric took a crack at him, and missed. He was chagrined, but I told him we all missed once in a while, and besides it was the first time he had used the 30-30. He said, "That's no excuse, Dad. We better check the gun out, but it's probably on and I was off."

Just a mile from our campsite, out on the wide open plain, we saw some movement under a small bush standing alone in the glare. Two mature leopards had moved from the shade of the bush and were loping slowly across the plain, now perhaps a qaurter of a mile away from us. They ran easily, occasionally stopping to watch our approach. I slowed down, and they stopped, tails flicking lazily but every muscle poised. I speeded up and they took off at nearly top speed. Ramadhani Kamata urged me to shoot one of them, but I informed him I did not have the necessary license. He accepted this calmly, although Eric did not. He wanted me to get one of them and then get the special permit. This I would not do. I *would* do it without hesitation if it were a matter of life and death to me or one of my party, and then I would try to get a license so as to keep the skin.

We didn't often see two leopards together. They are solitary animals, roaming their territory alone except during the mating season. I do not know of any definitive studies which have determined just how much territory one leopard will ordinarily claim as his own, but it must be somewhere in the neighborhood of ten to twenty square miles. They will move through this territory, staying for a week or two in an area, then move on to another place within their claim. Periodically we saw signs of a leopard on our mission station, tracks in the road or crossing our gardens, and once Edna* and I saw one in the tree just outside our house. But then the sightings and the tracks would cease, and it would be another month or two before the leopard returned. The first evidence of his return was usually a stolen goat or dog from some farmer's yard, and then we knew that for a week or two we could expect to see tracks or hear about sightings. One of the missionary nurses, Alice Turnbladh, saw one on her back porch one night when she returned home from the hospital, and one of the African medical assistants saw one lying on the ground outside his house.**

The two leopards we were following across the open plain disappeared in the trees, and we turned aside to go toward our campsite. We dropped off our camping gear, rested for a half hour or so, and then started out to hunt. It was about two o'clock when we returned to

* Edna – the author's wife.
** Dr. Don Rude shot a leopard inside the house of a hospital cook two months after we left Kiomboi, presumably the same one that had been around our compound for so long.

the track we had followed in, and drove for about five miles through rather dense bush without seeing anything. Coming to a wide swamp, we determined quickly that there was still too much water in it for us to cross, so we zeroed in the two guns, finding, as Eric had predicted, that they both were "on target."

A few minutes later Nosoro spotted a herd of wildebeest, and we followed them slowly through the bush until they joined up with a herd of zebra and stopped to watch us. The zebra spooked when we stopped the car, but the wildebeest held their ground long enough for me to get out and get well hidden. Eric drove the Land-Rover about a half a mile away and I started my stalk. I was about 300 yards away when I began, and was able to get up to about 200 yards by keeping bushes and trees between me and the 'beests, but then I found it necessary to get down on hands and knees for the final hunt. I wasn't sure how close I could get, but I wanted to narrow the distance to about 150 yards if I could. The ground was as hard as rock and my knees were beginning to rub raw when I finally decided I was as close as I was going to get. I hunched down behind a small bush to catch my breath and to wipe the perspiration out of my eyes. The herd was edgy, some of them starting to move off, but several stood broadside to me, watching in my direction, sensing danger. I was sure they hadn't seen me, and the wind was blowing directly from them to me, so I waited patiently until I was steady. I figured the distance at about 140 yards when I lined up and levelled my iron sights on the shoulder of one of the gray-blue beasts. He went down in a heap, and I walked slowly toward him, listening to the roar of the Land-Rover as Eric came up from behind the bush where he had concealed himself and the car. He went on past me, and Ramadhani leaped out of the car when they reached the wildebeest, and ritually cut his throat so that he and Nosoro could eat the meat.

We left two men with the kill, followed after the zebra, but they had put too much bush between them and us, and we never saw them again. We returned to the kill, loaded it aboard, and headed back for camp. A lone Tommy ram stood ahead of us in the grass at the edge of the open plain, and Eric dropped him with one shot from his 30-30 at a distance of 160 yards. A beautiful shot, I thought to myself as I paced off the distance while Eric drove up to the gazelle. Not bad for a thirteen-year-old boy. It made up for the clean miss on the impala.

Much has been written about the disappearing game in East Africa, some of it true and some of it nonsense. It is true that in parts of East Africa which once teemed with game there have been reductions in game populations, but some people have an erroneous idea about the cause. A decrease in the number of animals comes about in several ways: encroachment of civilization, hunting, and poaching.

By far the most important is the encroachment of civilization; sport hunting has a negligible effect, and poaching has a sporadic, isolated effect. Most of the game animals in East Africa are what I call the "wilderness animals," animals which either cannot or have not yet adapted themselves to living close to humans. We have their counterparts in the States: the brown bear, polar bear, elk, snowshoe rabbit, and the wolf. Many other animals, such as the cottontail rabbit and the deer, have not only adapted themselves to humans but seem to thrive on this association. Deer, for instance, have never been more populous in my home state of Wisconsin than they are today.*

* Why? Their numbers vary directly with the supply of grass, grains, and browse (tips of bushes and deciduous tree branches). When Wisconsin was covered with dense coniferous forests which did not allow for the growth of those deerfoods, the population was correspondingly low. But as the pines were lumbered out, farms carved out of the forest, there was a gradually increasing amount of food,

In Africa, few of the animals have yet adapted themselves to human settlements, so when a new farm is cut out of the bush, there are three or four acres less for those animals to live in. When roads open up an area, people move in, and the animals move out. Fortunately for the game, the population explosion has not yet found its way to East Africa, and there are only a relatively few areas into which people have moved in sufficient numbers to affect the survival of game in that area. There are vast parts of Tanzania which have not changed, and will not change for decades, as far as population density is concerned. There are approximately 12,000,000 people living in a country with an area of 362,000 square miles. For comparison, consider that the United States has a population of about 200 million, and has an area of just over 3,600,000 square miles, or twenty times the number of people and only ten times the area of Tanzania. Or to look at it another way: Illinois has about the same population as Tanzania, but has only 56,000 square miles in which to house them.

What occupies the unpeopled lands? Animals. Uncounted millions of them. Now I do not want to understate the problem of conservation, for it is a real one in terms of future generations, and it is an important one now for certain species of animals which are relatively rare and becoming rarer — rhino, for instance, which now must be protected in Tanzania to prevent extinction. Furthermore, poachers in and around the major game reserves are taking huge numbers of elephants for their ivory, and an illegal cache of almost 2,000 zebra skins was recently uncovered near Arusha.

But the fact still remains that in Tsavo National Park (on the Kenya-Tanzania border) a controlled killing of elephants became necessary in 1966 when the herd grew to 20,000 in an area of 10,000 square miles, twice

and the number of deer have increased accordingly, from an estimated half million in 1850 to ten million now.

the number that conservationists calculated could continue to live there without imperiling the maintenance of other species. The fact also remains that in the back country (75 percent) of Tanzania, thousands of elephants still roam along the watercourses, giant herds of zebra, wildebeest, and eland graze the plains, and impala, reedbuck, wildpig and hartebeest survive with ease in the forests.

So when one speaks of the disappearing game in East Africa, he must be careful to pinpoint the problem, which is this: there must be planning now, by this generation, to ensure that 1) large tracts of land remain in the province of the game conservationists, so that when the population does expand and when farms become bigger there will be places for the animals to live in comparative safety, and 2) the species which are now overhunted for their horns or tusks or hides will be properly protected.

Our campsite was idyllic. The tent was set up beside a huge old baobab tree about a stone's throw from a small water hole. The water was brownish in color, but clear, and a few lily pads grew around the edges. Two great blue herons were stalking frogs when we drove up and they flapped away in panic, only to return an hour later when our camp settled down. All around us were the umbrella trees (acacias), graceful and green, even in the dry season. Our camp in order, we left two men to dress out the Tommy and collect firewood, and Nosoro and Eric and Ramadhani and I went out to hunt. It was only about four P.M., which left us two good hours of daylight. We had a lot of mouths to feed at home and wanted to get four or five animals to take back with us to Kiomboi.

Within fifteen minutes Eric spotted a herd of about 100 eland standing in an open grassland a quarter of a mile away. They were wary of us, and I could only get within about 200 yards of them in the Land-Rover. Eland are big antelopes, running up to 1800 pounds, and perhaps the best eating of the plains game. I shot at one big bull, knew I had hit him by the way he acted, and followed on foot as the herd thundered off. Ramadhani and I tracked that herd for almost an hour and a half, and never came up to them again. I was convinced that I had scored, but apparently it had not been anything more than a muscle wound, and we lost him. On our way back to the Land-Rover, we came across a small herd of impala, also too wary to get close to, but since they were headed toward Eric and Nosoro, we followed them slowly. Trailing the herd was a lone hartebeest, and soon I heard Eric's 30-30 ring out, and when we came up to the car Eric was proudly cleaning out the hartebeest. We field-dressed the *kongoni* and went on.

It was just getting dusk when we kicked up a trio of buck impala. They bounded away, their graceful bodies reflecting the red of the setting sun, then stood to watch us from about seventy-five yards away. Eric leaped out of the car, shot off-hand, and one of the impala went down with a thud, only to leap up and take off as if he weren't even hit. Eric followed him beautifully and fired again, this time connecting in the neck, which is by far the best place to take any antelope.

We arrived back in camp a few minutes later, and Eric accepted the congratulations of the Africans with good grace. Godson Makala, our gardener and a young lad not much older than Eric, was particularly enthusiastic. I knew that Godson appreciated the skill involved in taking an antelope with a good clean shot, for he had learned by experience. One time as we were riding along with Eric on the roof shooting birds, Godson came up with one of his rare sentences in English, which he probably had been practicing for days: "Doctor, I want to beat." It took me just a moment to grasp his meaning.

Swahili has a word, "*kupiga,*" which means literally

"to beat," but it is one of those useful words found in all languages which also has many other connotations. *Kupiga mtu* does mean "to beat a man," but *kupiga magoti* means to get down on your knees such as to pray; *kupiga hodi* means to announce your presence outside a house and ask to come in; and when one is hunting the word means "to shoot." So when Godson translated his own phrase "*Nataka kupiga*" into English, it came out "I want to beat," since he apparently didn't know the word "shoot." So I put him out on the hood with the shotgun and showed him how to use it. He had strict orders to keep the gun pointed out in front of him at all times. We drove along slowly, spotted a flock of *kanga* skittering off into the bush, followed them, and Godson started to shoot. He missed every time, of course, and after he had shot up about a dollar's worth of good shells he signalled me to stop. He climbed down off the spare tire, handed me the gun, climbed back into the Land-Rover without a word, and never asked "to beat" again! The other Africans in the car were doubled over with laughter but I stopped that with just one question, "Does anyone else want to try?" There were no takers, but there was a much increased appreciation for Eric's shooting ability when he picked off *kanga* running erratically through heavy bush at thirty miles an hour, or coolly dropped them out of the air while clinging precariously to a moving Land-Rover!

The Tommy had been cut up into edible parts, and while the Africans cooked their meat by laying it on the open fire, we fried some steaks in the frying pan, heated some soup, boiled some coffee, and had the finest supper you can imagine. The vultures in the trees were settling down for the night and a few rods away a wildcat screeched periodically far into the night. There were the usual night sounds as we sat around the campfire, the conversation alternately in English when Nosoro and Eric and I were talking, or Swahili when any of us were conversing with the Africans.

What does one talk about on such a night? About the leopards we had seen loping across the plains, and how someday we might try to get one. About the lions which might come right into our camp, the ones that you didn't even need a "bite" for. About the .458 that Nosoro wanted me to get for him when I returned to the States in six months. About the shotgun which Nosoro wanted to buy from me when it arrived from the States (I did eventually get it a few days before I left Kiomboi, and I did sell it to him). About plans for the next day's hunt. With the Tommy nearly gone, we had three animals to take home. They were strung up in a nearby tree, high enough that the hyenas could not get at them. A hyena cannot stand on his hind legs without a brace for his front legs, so the meat had to be only about three feet off the ground.

It was a black, moonless night, but the fire was comforting, the coffee hot, and the talk exhilarating. There was no thought of danger. I don't ever recall being worried about depredations of man or beast; I only mention it because so many people say, "Weren't you scared to death, sleeping out there in the bush, with all those wild animals around?" The answer is: no. We took routine precautions such as putting all food in the Land-Rover, for that might provoke a hyena to try to get into a tent. We never slept outside the tent, because of the danger of a prowling hyena taking a bite out of our faces, but even that is a minimal danger, and I know many people who sleep in the open more or less routinely when they are out in the bush.

There was a sliver of a moon in the east when we got up before dawn the next morning and a hush hung over the bush. The only interruption of our night's sleep had been the close-by snorting of a curious impala who circled our camp slowly, blowing like a deer every twenty to thirty seconds. I say impala because although

I didn't see it, it is the only animal except for the deer whom I have ever heard make that rather characteristic sound.

A new day had come, but no one yet knew what to do with it. To move fast, or talk loudly, or rattle the coffee pot seemed somehow sacrilegious in a hallowed hour. So I stepped outside my tent, nodded to the Africans squatted by the fire eating some more flame-roasted gazelle meat, splashed a little unboiled water onto my face, combed my hair and in a voice like a whisper said, "*Habari gani asubuhi hii?*" (What's the news this morning?") A chorus of "*Nzuri tu, bwana daktari*" (Just good, sir doctor) broke open the lock on the day, and I called, "Come on, Eric, it's daylight in the swamp!" The grayness of the cold morning disappeared in the red ball of a sun rising above the yellow plains and we saw a long string of zebra slowly wending their way across the grasslands a half mile away. We heated up the coffee and ate some of Edna's homemade (what else?) sweet rolls. Their meal over, the Africans in the party brushed their teeth with the frayed ends of soft green twigs, so I had to brush mine too. The day was now here. Let's go.

We piled into the Land-Rover and took off down the track toward the open plains where Eric had gotten the Tommy the day before. Impala bounded ahead of us and off to both sides, caught napping in the early light, but there were no bucks of sufficient size to hunt. *Kwale* (partridge-sized birds) and *kanga* (wild guinea fowl) ran or flushed ahead of us, but we were more interested in bigger game. A hyena circled ahead of us and came to a wary point fifty yards in the bush; we were not interested in him either. He could tell it and held his ground. We circled the square mile of open plains and with some surprise noted they were devoid of game. We hunted vainly for about two hours and then went back to camp for some bacon and eggs and more coffee. While Eric and Godson and I struck camp, Ramadhani and Nosoro loaded the impala and *kongoni* on the car-rack behind the tent, and then we all loaded the wildebeest inside the car. The Land-Rover was getting bloodier and bloodier, inside and out, and a few flies had found a good spot to lay their eggs and were crawling over the meat.

We took one more swing out through the acacias to the west of our camp and came on one of the biggest wild boars I have ever seen. He had gotten big by being fast and wary, and Eric had to take a long shot at him while he angled away from us on his short stubby legs, his tufted tail straight up in the air like a kid balancing a broom on one finger. The first shot got him in the back leg, and within a few minutes we were up to him and put him away with a .22 bullet in the head. He was a monster. His weight was close to three hundred pounds, and his tusks (the upper canines) measured fourteen inches on each side. Not thinking quickly enough, I forbade Nosoro and Ramadhani to cut its throat in the ritual Muslim manner, knowing that we would then have even more blood all over the place. But then we had an even greater problem: what to do with the pig so that its uncleanness would not contaminate the rest of the meat that *had* been ritually killed. We came to a reluctant decision. We untied the impala and *kongoni* and put them inside with the wildebeest, making an awful pile of meat, and then laboriously pulled the pig up on top, lashing it down so it wouldn't fall off when we hit an ant-bear hole or a dried-up elephant track.

All of us had had enough hunting except Eric, and he sat on the spare tire on the hood as we drove back to Mduguyu, shooting *kanga* and *kwale* with the .410 shotgun. Edna loved for us to bring back birds because she could use them for all kinds of hot dishes rather than use the tough little chickens she would have to pressure-cook before using. One dish she made was a favorite of ours: *kwale* and cubes of bread that she browned in the oven. She never makes it at home; probably there are too many other good ways to use the tender chickens we can obtain in the States.

We left Ramadhani and his friend at the *gundi* village, promising to leave a couple of antelope legs at his *boma* when we went by. Then just outside the village we came across Nosoro's son in Nosoro's Land-Rover. They had just met an elephant in the road, and before I knew it, Nosoro was gone, too, hot on the trail. We learned later that he had failed to find it. Our hunting party had dwindled to Eric and Godson and myself and we followed the trail on through the bush to Ramadhani's *boma,* dropped off some meat for his wife (wives?) to divide up with the rest of the clan, and started the long climb to the top of the escarpment, the sun now directly overhead and beginning to burn.

I don't suppose many clients of White Hunters would call our twenty-four hour excursion a real safari, compared to what they were used to, but we had had fun, we had gotten some meat for our station, and we had left the *mbuga* in very much the same condition in which we had found it. Perhaps a part of Africa goes home with those men who come for two weeks, and perhaps they have time to sit by the campfire and absorb a little of the magnetism that emanates from the bush. But knowing that we could come again and again into the quietness of the wilderness gave us an opportunity to sit down and think – to appreciate what was ours. We were *there,* we lived in the country, and we could think more deeply about it. We knew it would remain a part of us, down in the secret places of our restless hearts, soothing, beguiling, somewhat elusive, but always, always, calling us back.

8 / Paulo Zakaria

It was a time of hunger. Hunger of the belly kind that draws the fat from the skin so that it crinkles loosely over the muscles, and sucks the protein from the tissues so that fluid collects in the legs of the adults and in the protruding abdomens of the children. Hunger that cannot be assuaged by a few tablespoons of *uji* in the morning and a few handfuls of *ugale* in the evening.

We had come into Isanzu country, about forty miles from Kiomboi. The area was in the grip of a long drought and the land was seared. It was now the normal time for the dry season, but four months before, the rainy season had ended too soon, leaving unripened corn to burn on the stalk, beans to curl into little finger-fitting rings, and peanut plants to fall to earth before the legumes could fructify. The winds roared day and night, flicking burning embers from the campfires into the unharvested millet.

So now the grass was yellow, the mountains brown and bleak except where a green-gray euphorbia fingered the sky with its tentacles, dust flew across the roads and fields, and it was a time of hunger. Nothing would grow. No one even tried to plant anything for they knew it was futile and it made more sense to eat the seeds. The men sat in the shade of their houses or under the trees, or walked about aimlessly; the women sat in their doorways or against the mudwalls preparing the evening meal in the big black pot. A few children played listlessly in the blowing dust.

Water. The word rang like a gong in my head. What these people needed was water. They could get enough to drink from the dry river bed, digging down through a foot or two of sand until cold water seeped into the hole, but the clay ground a few feet away lay cracked and parched.

We had driven east across the tip of our plateau to Kinampanda, down the steep escarpment into the valley of the Ndurumo River, across the old concrete bridge that lay alongside the crumbled remains of an even older wood and stone bridge, up the valley to Msingi, along the floor of the valley through Gumanga to the foot of the Isanzu Mountains. A winding, sandy road carried us upward, high into the mountaintop town of Mkalama. On the highest peak an old fort lay in ruins, a reminder that before World War I the Germans ruled this part of the world. In the courtyard there still stands the giant old baobab tree. Vultures came to it to pick clean the Africans who were hung there as an example to the populace that they must obey the laws of their colonial rulers.

Then down the other side of the ridge the road rambled, across another dry wash impassable in the rainy season, and finally into the mountains of the Waisanzu.* Abruptly the road started climbing along a narrow track which resembled a waterless mountain streambed more than it did a road. On both sides we

* Pronounced wah-ee-san'zu.

began to see huge granite boulders jutting up into the sky for 50 or 100 or 150 feet, creating fantastic shapes that invited our imagination to give them names. We climbed up and over a succession of ridges, each higher than the preceding one, from whose tops we could see the sweep of boulder-strewn ridges and valleys.

Dense bush closed in, thorn trees scratched along the sides of the Land-Rover, acacias spread their umbrellas overhead, and now and then the passage was guarded by a 2,000-year-old baobab, seemingly upside down with its roots high in the air and its branches pushed by the devil deep into the desiccated earth. At 5,000 feet we reached a mesa-like ridge, and spewed dust from our wheels as we turned into the short driveway of Rev. Bob Ward's home.

The house was big, rambling, ranch-like, with a porch running more than half-way around the house. The porch came right off an Iowa farm: it held bulk food supplies, cream separator, boots, garden implements, raincoats, and endless other items used in country living.

Waiting for supper, Bob and I sat in his "study," more a workroom than anything. One whole side of the room was filled with radio boxes and gear – I counted eight separate machines for receiving, transmitting, testing – and in one corner were four elephant tusks, spears, bows and arrows, rifles, while in another corner was a pile of radios sent to him by friends for repair.

I brought up the subject of the drought. "Isn't there some way these people could get more water, Bob?" I asked.

"Not now. They'll have to tough this one out. Food is being shipped from all over, up from your area where the rains were good last year, from government stores, from mission supplies. But there *is* a way to prevent all this."

"There is? Then in heaven's name why hasn't it been done?"

"It's a long story. Want to hear it? A shortened version of it, that is?" he grinned mischievously.

"Sure, and don't shorten it unnecessarily. I love to hear stories." I *do,* too, especially when Bob Ward tells them. I rocked back in my chair, put my feet up on his desk where they vied for room with his books, Bibles, papers, and the other paraphernalia of a man who has never had a clean desk in his life.

Well, (he began), this is the story of Paulo Zakaria, a classic story of a man with a dream. Paulo is about thirty, a first generation Christian, lean and hard like all the Waisanzu. Uneducated, of course. Came along a little too late to get in on either the missionary or government attempts to educate the kids. But he's clever, real clever, and he thinks. Dreams, too, which immediately sets him off a little from the mainstream.

One day in the dry season, about two years ago, he was walking through a nearby valley that has become completely unpopulated because the soil has been badly overworked and now doesn't support crops. That valley is full of wild pigs and leopards. Only things that live there. The pigs eat the vegetation and the leopards eat the pigs. You might say that whole valley and the surrounding mountain range is just saturated with leopards. They roam quite a bit, too, you know, so the natives who are too lazy or too ignorant to build a tight *boma* get into trouble every once in a while because a leopard will come in at night and carry off a youngster or a goat or a calf.

Paulo was sort of dreaming that day. He remembered how just a few months before the water had roared down that valley, and the bush was green and lush. In the farmed areas, crops grew rapidly: corn and millet and peanuts and beans. Their chief had really outdone himself that year, bringing rains that promised an abundance of food to last them through the next dry season.

But where, Paulo wondered, where was all that water now? Where did it go when it rushed off down the hillside? Was it still running down there somewhere, bringing life-giving water to some other people? Or did it just soak into the ground like a mud-puddle? There must be some way to keep all that water around so they could use it. There must be an answer, but he knew he didn't have it.

Back in his village he began talking to the other men about the water.

"What do you mean, Paulo, we've got to do something about the water?" they asked incredulously.

"Well, I mean we've got to find some way to keep some of all that rain water and river water here in our mountains after the rains stop."

They looked at him askance, uncomprehending, completely unable to grasp any thread of meaning.

"Why," they said, "our Chief brings rain every year. We grow enough crops to feed us for the next year. What more do you want?"

"I want water *all* year."

"*Mjingo,*" they hurled in his face and stalked off.

Crazy man. *Yes, I guess I am,* he thought.

But something kept nagging at him. He knew he wasn't crazy. Maybe he had a crazy idea, but then again what was so crazy about wanting to grow corn twelve months of the year? There was sun and warmth all year round, but water for only half the year. Even in the best of years they never really had too much to eat, and when the rains failed – they starved.

He brooded, and pondered, and walked all day in the dry countryside and along the dusty riverbeds. The idea grew in his mind that there were two ways to grow crops all year. One was to have rain all year. This had never happened, and he couldn't remember the reason for it. Something to do with the inadequate powers of even the most powerful chiefs and medicine men. But God was all-powerful, wasn't He? Maybe if the whole congregation prayed real hard every day? But of course they had tried that several times when there was the threat of too little rain during the rainy season. Sometimes it seemed to work and sometimes it didn't.

The second way was to trap that water somehow—not let it get away. Dam it up. The thought staggered him. One would have to fill the whole valley from one side to the other with rocks and dirt. And then how would you get it to the fields? He had no answer, and was despondent.

In the following weeks the idea gradually faded from his mind, and when he talked less and less of his dreams, he was reaccepted by his tribesmen. It was a hollow triumph.

In September black clouds began to gather in the eastern skies toward afternoon of every day. The rains were coming. In the bush the bright red flowers began to sprout alongside the acacia trees, the *jacarandas* showed signs of life as the tiny purple flowers began to open even before the first rain, and in countless other ways Paulo witnessed again the strange phenomenon of the bush preparing itself for the coming of the rains.

The people became restless, easily irritated, prone to argument. Fights broke out and knives and *pangas* flashed. Suicides increased alarmingly; Paulo's brother-in-law was found hanging in a dry well, three days after he disappeared. You probably did the post-mortem on him, Birney; we sent him to Kiomboi in the Game Ranger's car. (I didn't remember the specific case, but I did know that crimes of violence and suicides shot up toward the end of the dry season.)

Then one day, instead of clouding up temporarily, the blackness rolled out over the land and the rainy season began. From that day on, for nearly six months, it rained almost every day: hard, bruising rains that lashed the ground with whips of wind-blown fury. Between storms the sun shone hot and the crops and bush grew gloriously green.

Paulo Zakaria walked out along the same valley that he had followed six months before. He saw the roaring river, fed by an infinite number of rivulets and streamlets from the mountains and ridges. *It was the same old story,* he thought: *too much water now, so that it rushes off and is lost, while in just a few months we will be parched and dry again.*

He swung around to the east, began climbing toward the village of Isanzu a mile away. The sun was low in the west behind him, throwing dark shadows into the deeply yellow rocks on the ridge behind the town. On the highest point a white cross shone brightly, thrown into relief by the black clouds of still another storm. As he watched, a rainbow began to take shape against the clouds, and in a few moments it arched high into the sky, its lower end buried in the granite at the base of the cross.

It could be nothing but an omen. But what did it mean? His mind rambled through several of the superstitions he had heard over the years, but these he discarded in favor of a more obvious answer. The man who had put the cross up there was the man to talk to about saving the water.

He scrambled up here to see me as fast as his legs could carry him. I can still see him standing there at the back door, face dripping with sweat and rainwater, knees and hands bruised and bleeding from fighting through the brush. His *kanzu,* normally white, was dirty and torn. His breathless "*Hodi*" had sounded from at least 100 feet away, so that I was calling "*Karibu*" almost before he got to the door! He was a sight, but I invited him in and he sat here in this room. As a matter of fact, he was sitting right where you are, but he didn't have the temerity to put his feet up on my desk!

He told me quickly what had happened. Now I don't know just how you feel about these things, Birney, but I also took his experience as a direct message from God. He had been sent to me by means of a sign. I can see you're a little unconvinced. Well, anyway, I listened to his story, and although I pretended to weigh his problem for the proper length of time, the solution was so obvious that I was surprised that it hadn't been done before. Paulo had been right – what they needed was a dam. As I described how it could be done, Paulo sat as if mesmerized, his eyes wide and almost glowing in the subdued light of the late afternoon.

The next day we held a meeting out in the gorge – all the men of the surrounding area came – and I showed them how they could dam up the river during the dry season so that they would have a big reservoir to fill during the next rainy season. I showed them how they could run irrigation ditches out from the flowage to feed water into the fields. Almost everyone was enthused about the project. Except the Chief. He stood back in the shade of an acacia tree, arms folded on his chest, eyes half-closed, unmoved by all the excitement around him. Some of the tribal elders glanced at him occasionally to see how he was reacting and what they saw wasn't good. Slowly I realized that I had made a colossal goof. I should have known better. There wasn't a chance of the project getting off the ground unless the Chief gave his o.k., and that would never happen unless he had thought of it, or at least unless it could be made to appear as if he had thought of it.

I withdrew from the center of the discussion, leaving the men to talk it out. Out of the corner of my eye I saw an elder in earnest conversation with the Chief, and then the elder returned to the circle.

"Listen," he said. "I'm opposed to this plan for one good reason. This land that you propose to submerge is sacred ground to many people. Think of all the people who have lived here and died here, long years ago, and who are buried in this valley. Are you going to bury them under a flood of water so that their relatives cannot come and venerate them any longer? And what of the gods who live in the stones and the trees which will be drowned by your stupid project? Will they not react in a violent way? Perhaps stop the rains entirely so that we will get no water at all, much less in this backwater you call a reservoir? No, I am completely opposed."

It was a good try, but it was not enough. He was shouted down by many men who pointed out the foolishness of his arguments. No one, they said, ever came to this valley anymore to pray to their ancestors. There were too many leopards to be safe. And as for the gods in the stones and trees (if there are indeed such things) they can find other homes if they are good gods, and will quite properly be drowned if they are bad gods.

The elder retired in some confusion, since it had not been his idea in the first place. The talk went on, and it seemed to me that some concrete plans might actually develop right there on the spot.

I sat on the sidelines watching the Chief. He was not through yet. Slowly he opened his eyes and walked into the center of the convocation. The discussion ceased.

"There will be no dam. It is not in the best interest of this tribe. Does anyone dare argue?"

I was pleased to see that there were several who dared. Younger men, of course, who still had the spirit to protest arbitrary pronouncements, and who had more years of hand-to-mouth living ahead of them than the older men. Paulo was one of them, and I was proud of him as he stood to summarize the advantages the dam would bring to all the people in the whole region.

I could sense the Chief wavering just a little and

wondered if the tribesmen could feel it too. They could. The pressure became intense. The Chief stood immobile, still in the center of the seated men, listening, alert, eyes moving from speaker to speaker, then out around the quietly brooding older men. I could see that soon he would have to move in one direction or the other. I prayed that it would be toward Paulo's side.

The last argument had been made. The last speaker sat down. The Chief leaned forward on his walking stick, his face now immutable. The roar of the water in the gorge below was the only sound I could hear except for the beating of my heart. Paulo squatted on his heels a few yards from me, his eyes staring straight upward into the face of his Chief. Slowly the Chief turned his head toward Paulo, recognizing him as his chief antagonist. Their eyes met boldly, then the Chief's gaze slowly searched the crowd, and I knew who he was looking for. And he found me.

"Haifai," he said sonorously, *"haitakuwa boma la kuzuia maji."* (It is no good. There will be no dam.)

He turned and stalked off. I learned later that he felt insecure enough that he had to promise work for all able-bodied men on a project of his own, followed by three years of no work at all, to keep peace in the tribe. Besides, he reminded them, he could stop the rains even in the rainy season. The combination of wanting to please their Chief in his project and not having to work for three years was too much. The dam was never built.

Paulo took it hard. He sat on his heels for an hour or more before he started back to the village. A storm came up and he sought refuge in a sort of cave — I'll show it to you tomorrow if there's time — not actually a cave, but an open space under a huge rock about seventy-five feet in diameter that is supported on several sides by other rocks so that one can walk in under it. He stood quietly, thinking, looking at the faded red

Isanzu country — "huge granite boulders jutting up into the sky."

paintings that had been drawn many centuries before by people who had lived in the cave and who had died or moved on to another place. There was a giraffe, a rhino, an eland, and a whole host of stick men throwing spears and shooting arrows at the animals. *These ancestors of mine,* he thought, *they lived and died here, struggling more than I do, no doubt, and still they survived. They survived by obeying the laws of nature, not by flouting them, and they obeyed their Chief.*

There were three shallow depressions alongside the figure of one stick-man. Generations of hunters had worn grooves in the rock by placing their fingers in the prints of one of their great hunters. In this way they had shown respect for their hero, had gained some of his strength and luck, and had shown obeisance to the traditions of their tribe.

Slowly Paulo Zakaria reached out and placed his fingers in the prints.

9 / Phillip Luo

Blindly we scaled the mountain, following the scandent, serpentine, sand strip that hugged the steep slope. Although near midday, our bright lights were on, the fog eddying and sifting around us, weird draperies of moss hanging eerily from the rain-forest trees. A truck lumbered down at us out of the whiteness, its lights weak as candles, and we forced ourselves over to the ditch, hoping he would see us in time and do the same; he did, and passed with inches to spare. The road leveled off after a climb of 5,000 feet, and somewhere down to the right was the floor of the largest and deadest unflooded volcanic caldera in the world – the Ngorongoro Crater – unseen in the swirling mists. We pushed on, hoping we wouldn't meet a Cape buffalo in the road, or an elephant, or even another truck. We felt rather than saw the road begin to drop again, slowly at first, then faster and faster, dropping off the west side of the rim of the crater, while the fog lifted, or rather stayed where it was while we descended.

We broke out of the humid air hovering on the outer slopes of the Crater and saw far below us a brilliant green bowl scattered with zebra, wildebeest and multicolored Masai cattle. The road curved around the bowl, clung to the edge, dropping lower and lower, and finally pushed through a corner of it onto the dry brown desolation of the thorn-tree hills above the Plains of Serengeti. We looked behind us and saw that the high mountain which contains the Crater was almost invisible in the fog, while ahead of us the air was clear except for the fine haze of dust and smoke that hangs over the land during the dry season. Off to the left towered the intensely green rounded peak of Lemagrut.

Long sloping gravel tracks, hairpin turns, crackling dry grass, whistling thorns, acacia forest, an occasional Thomson's or Grant's gazelle skipping across the road, a dip through a dry wash — this was the scene for the next half hour as we dropped rapidly and dustily onto the Serengeti. Long before we moved out onto the plains we could see the endlessness of it. Not a tree stood. Not a hill marked the tracklessness. The sun was directly overhead and the shadows fell helplessly at our feet. There was no way to tell East from West, North from South.

The miles went by as the dust floated upward into the air behind the Land-Rover. A gash of green appeared on the right, the dark green trees lining the edges of the Olduvai Gorge, site of the archaeological digs of Dr. Louis Leakey.

All at once there was a hill in the distance. An hour later we reached it, the sun hotter than ever, the dust drifting into the Land-Rover, the breeze redolent with the scent of tall dry grasses, the heat building up behind our sunglasses so that we had to take them off to wipe our eyes and then the white-yellow glare of the road and plain rending our vision until we put them back on again. We drank from the red plastic water jug: hot water, but wet, and we couldn't keep thermos bottles from breaking.

There was no human life on those plains. Tommies and Grant's fed across the yellow grass as far as the eye could see, but there were no wildebeest or zebras and we pondered the awesome spectacle we once witnessed on this road, when there were thousands upon thousands of wildebeest and zebras in this same area, migrating in response to ancient instinct, following the water in an endless circle of the Serengeti.

Then we met a man. He stood at the little "guardhouse" on the summit of the hill we had seen in the distance. His outstretched arm pumped slowly up and down in the classic African entreaty to stop. The Land-Rover floated to a stop in the cloud of dust that caught up with us and enveloped the car and the man.

We got out to stretch our legs as the man and I exchanged greetings in the traditional manner.

"*Jambo, bwana,*" he said. "*Habari ya safari?*" (How is your trip?)

"*Nzuri, bwana. Lakini moto sana.*" (Good, sir, but very hot.)

"*Ndio, bwana.*" (Yes, sir.)

We chatted for a few moments as I got a bucket of water to fill the boiling radiator. The heat pressed down around us and the ennui was almost overwhelming. It was all I could do to lift the hood of the car with its heavy spare wheel mounted on it. The metal burned my hand only slightly less than the radiator cap and the escaping steam was scarcely hotter than the air around me. Edna and the children stood in the shade of a tree beside the guardhouse, and gazelles stood curiously fifty yards away, chewing their cuds.

I could sense the loneliness of the African man and since we were in no hurry and rather welcomed a break, we drew aside into the shade and talked for a half hour or more. His name was Phillip Luo and he was an Mtaita, that is, a man of the Wataita tribe, and originally had lived in his tribal area in southern Kenya. From his name I knew he was Christian and he informed me that "most" of Wataita were Christian. He had gone to a mission grade school for five years, but had to drop out because of inability to pay the school fees.

He had had such a poor knowledge of geography that he had crossed the Kenya-Tanganyika border without even knowing it and had had all kinds of trouble getting a job with the Park Service because he did not hold Tanganyikan citizenship. But he had gotten the job, and had been in the Serengeti for nine years without ever leaving it, except for a trip to the Crater. I was not particularly surprised by his immobility. Rural people in general, the world around, and Africans in particular, do not travel because they have no money and they literally have no desire or need to go anywhere.

He was a small, lean man, with typically Bantu features and a closely cropped head of black hair. I liked him immediately, and promised to stop for a longer time on our return trip. Suddenly he started speaking English with a surprisingly good command of the tongue. I broke off into English, too, somewhat startled.

"Where did you learn such good English?"

"I start to speak in school. Standard Five, you know. Then I got a book, you know, from Standard Six. I studied good and sharp. Missionaries came by here, gave me books. I have taught myself." He grinned broadly.

"You certainly have taught yourself well," I said.

"*Ngoja kidogo,*" he said. (Wait a minute.)

He ran into the guardhouse and came out with a book and some papers from which he had been studying, and together we went over his lessons for an hour. I am no *fundi ya Kiswahili* (expert in Swahili) but I knew more Swahili than he did English, so I was able to help him over some of the rough spots in his lessons. He told me that he had not had any help for more than two years, when someone else had stopped and done what I had. It was incredible.

We drove on after promising to stop on the way back. Ahead of us we saw an advancing grass fire, an experimental burn by game wardens trying to determine whether the animals would feed in the tall dry grass or in the burn. It was obvious to us that the tiny green shoots in the burned-over areas were preferred to the unburned plains. Smoke billowed into the air and flames shot up fifty feet as the wind drove the line eastward. In front of the fireline the plains were barren of game, but behind it huge birds wheeled in the air, dropping in behind the fire onto the scorched and still smoking earth. At the juncture of burned and unburned grass the road was blocked by hundreds of birds, mostly Maribou and European storks, bellies stuffed with their gleanings of blackened snakes, birds, lizards, and rodents which could not escape the inferno.

The sun was on the horizon when we approached Seronera, a tent-camp in the middle of the Serengeti. We crossed an almost dry river and saw giraffe standing stoically alongside it. A small reedbuck dropped to the ground so that all we could see were his short, forward-pointing horns. *Kwale* and *kanga* ran along the sand road ahead of us.

We registered in the little hut with the pointed grass roof, tourists milling around us, the first Americans we had seen for almost a year except for other missionaries. Most of them had come in from the north, traveling in mini-buses from Masai Mara in southwestern Kenya. We were hot and tired and dusty, but this was our life and we were used to it.

One of the Americans was not. His wife and two teen-age girls stood off to the side as the following exchange occurred.

"What the h--- does a guy have to do to get some

decent accommodations around here?" he said to the flurried African registrar.

"Sir?" the registrar queried, and I wondered how much English the fellow knew. I soon found out.

"I mean," the American continued, "we got reservations for two tents months ago, and now I find out that one of them is on one side of the camp and the other is clear over on the other side."

"I see," the African said quietly. "I'm very sorry, sir, but we were unable to put your two tents together, so I'm afraid you will have to separate. Perhaps you could sleep in one with one of your daughters and your wife could sleep in the other with the second daughter. That is, if you don't want the girls to sleep alone. I can tell you, however, that they will be perfectly safe alone."

"Perfectly safe? In the middle of the African jungle? Man, I wouldn't even let them sleep in a tent alone in the States, much less here."

"Sir, there are fifty tents here, with perhaps one hundred fifty people, and we have guards who patrol the whole camp all night. I can assure you. . . ."

"What I want is two tents next to each other. Don't you understand?"

"We cannot change the tents around now, but perhaps if you spoke to the people next to you, they would change with you."

"The h--- I will. That's your business. Do I get the tents or don't I?"

"I'm afraid not, sir."

"Well, who do I see . . . ?"

I walked outside. The air was cool and clean and the wind blowing in off the savanna carried a scent like new-mown hay. A half-moon rode high in the sky, tilted forward slightly as if to tip the old moon out of its grasp. As we drove the few yards to our own tent, I found it quite easy to forget about the Ugly American.

After supper, as we lay on our cots reading, a little

shower of rain drummed on the roof and then was gone. Hyenas roamed close, and their eerie calls reminded us of our own home 200 miles to the south. Eric and I doubled over in laughter as a young boy next door cried out, "Dad, that must have been an elephant!" and we resisted the temptation to call over to correct him. A cool breeze blew through the screened windows of the tent and we pulled blankets over us and fell asleep.

We were tourists, too, and in the early morning we were out in the Land-Rover, watching the plains shimmer with mirages as the heat began to build up. We drove slowly, watching the Tommies and giraffes, topis and impala. A big cat came loping across the grassland and I called, "It's a leopard," and was immediately corrected by my son. "*No,* it's a cheetah. And there's two more."

They stalked gracefully through the grass, small heads high and long thin bodies moving effortlessly, tails flicking aimlessly. One of them scratched his back on the front bumper of the Land-Rover. Hovering nearby were several dozen gazelles, some of them feeding, others watching unconcernedly as the cheetahs roamed freely on the open plain.

Suddenly, one of the cheetahs caught a scent. He raised up on his front feet, his rump carelessly draped on the ground, his eyes bright in the morning sun, the black tear-drops below his eyes clearly seen at the short distance of thirty or forty feet. His back feet came up under him as he strained for the scent, poised in midair, front shoulders hunched, muscles rippling gently as he maintained the half-crouch. Then we saw what the cheetah had smelled.

A half-grown Tommy stood mesmerized in the tall grass, his eyes mirroring the ancient fear of the hunted, his legs unable to carry him off. The cheetah did not move an inch or a muscle. The other two cheetahs joined the tableau, one of them stretched along the ground, the third sitting boldly upright. It was a motion picture, caught in temporary stop-action like an instant replay.

We looked at the Tommy again. Fear was written into every line of his body and we knew he wished he could fly. We also knew that we were witnessing in the cheetah the deliberate functioning of the most basic drive of them all – hunger. The drive that surpasses the instincts of gregariousness, of shelter-building, of sex, of self-preservation. We also were witnessing the expression of the law to which all creatures on earth bow – and which is nowhere better demonstrated than in Africa – the survival of the fittest. Man may fight over land. He may fight over religion. He may wage wars of aggression under the aegis of self-preservation. He may die with chauvinistic grace, soundlessly repeating the pounded-copper ideologies of long-dead "martyrs." But he will not necessarily die because he *isn't* the strongest, or the cleverest, or even the fittest. He may die idiotically with a steering wheel in his chest, or he may slip on a banana peel and break his neck, and no one will ever know whether he was the strongest, or the cleverest, or the fittest.

With the sure knowledge that for him all *that* is nonsense, the little Tommy decided that he must run or he must die . . . he made a single movement to turn and run. This triggered the chase instincts of the waiting cheetahs, and with the tremendous speed of which they are capable, the speed that ranks them as the fastest of all land animals, they streaked across the fifty yards that separated them from the Tommy, and like a well-trained team, they closed in and made the kill. The Tommy never had a chance.

The gruesomeness of the cat-and-mouse game stayed with us for a long time as we followed the dry river bed. In the bush, a redbrown impala watched us, stiff-legged, sloe-eyed like the American deer, lyre-shaped horns spiralling upwards; then he leaped high in the air, his does and young following in the same leaping, cavorting dance, a modern ballet set to some unrecognizable time. A mother pig and her three young knelt on the ground, digging roots, and when frightened they ran off jauntily with tufted tails ludicrously straight in the air like children with gas-filled balloons tied to their bikes. A female waterbuck watched covertly from dense foliage, her heavy brown coat camouflaging her perfectly in the shadows. Above her head, three vervet monkeys chattered, then leapt across the stream into another tree and scampered from branch to branch.

We came upon a huge leopard, belly slung low in the tall grass, eyes peering evilly from under hooded lids, legendary power only hinted at with each impassive step. Effortlessly he climbed a fever tree and draped himself along a branch a hundred feet or more in the air, all four extremities and tail hanging loosely.

A hundred yards away, two prides of lions lay listlessly in grass so tall that we almost missed seeing them. One young male had just the beginning of black tipping his mane and he looked every bit the heir to his segment of the wild kingdom. In truth, however, the king of the jungle is not the lion. He is no match for the Cape buffalo, nor the elephant, nor even the rhino, and he knows it. Knows it so well that he avoids putting his alleged kingship on the line where the myth might be destroyed.

An old lioness with the tuft missing from the tip of her tail sniffed the ground, pawed at it like a cat at a mousehole, then got up and walked so close to our Land-Rover that I felt as if I could reach out and pet her. Instead, I pulled back a little as she looked up at me from three feet away.

That night in the tent I felt again the mood of the Serengeti: peace. There are the carnivores, it is true, with their penchant for instilling instant terror, but it is purposeful, and it is only for an instant. The winds blew strongly, swaying the few trees along the watercourses and rippling the grasses like fields of wheat. It was a peaceful wind, steady and dependable; it is during the few periods when there is no wind that you feel restless and irritable and not at peace. The endless, open plains create an aura of serenity, appreciated by the city-dweller who lives in box canyons of claustrophobic concrete, but appreciated best by the plains-dweller who has had his life molded into patterns of freedom, his mind uncluttered by the fetters of clocks and appointments, luncheons and meetings, stresses and strains, ulcers and coronaries.

The following morning we drove back to Arusha, stopping at the Naabi Hills guardhouse to keep our rendezvous with Phillip Luo. As we approached, his arm began the up and down motion but ceased almost immediately as he recognized the car. His face broke into a thousand smiles.

"How do you do, sir?" he said in his best English.

"Very well, and you?"

"I am also very well, thank you."

He listened enraptured as we told him of the animals we had seen. I quickly lapsed into Swahili so he could get the full story without straining.

"And the leopard was very big, sir?" he asked.

"Very big. And he climbed the yellow fever tree as if it were a bush."

"I know. I have seen where they have carried an almost full-grown wildebeest up into a tree so they could eat it later."

"Yes, I have seen that, too."

"Do you not have wild animals in America?"

"Yes, some. Our biggest dangerous animal is the bear. Perhaps you have seen pictures of him? But we don't see him very often because he is afraid of men."

"How much I would like to go to America some day!"

"Perhaps you will."

"No, I don't think so. It is too far and costs too much money. And I haven't had enough education to go there to study."

"Yes, I suppose that is true. Most Africans in the U.S. are sent by the government or by missions."

"I have always liked Americans. They are always so friendly and helpful. Like you. They are not like the British who often pretend you are not even there unless they want you to do something unpleasant for them."

"I'm afraid that there are Americans who are not very nice, too," I said with a smile, remembering the tourist in the registrar's office at Seronera.

"I suppose so. But I have always admired America because it is a Christian country and everyone there is a Christian."

I started to argue with him again, but closed my mouth and listened in awe.

"Christian countries like America have been especially blessed by God, and this is the reason that everyone there is rich. If the people in a country are all Christian, they will all do God's will, and God will be good to them. You remember the Mau Mau? They were not Christian, and they went about the country killing everyone who disagreed with them. Mostly they killed other Africans, but they killed white people, too, some of whom were British and had taken their land and had treated them harshly, but some of them were missionaries or other white people who had only done them good. My tribe, the Wataita, did not join the Mau Mau, nor did the Wakamba, so we were killed, too. That could never happen in America."

"I do not like to spoil your fine picture of the Americans, Phillip, but we did fight each other, a hundred years ago, and we have had a long bitter fight to give all our people equal rights ever since."

"Oh, but that must have been different. One side must have been non-Christians. Yes, I'm sure it was different, or it would not have happened in America."

I could see he had a distorted picture of America, and nothing I could say would change it. I did try a few more times to break up his illusions, but he had his own ideas and didn't *want* to be disillusioned.

We rumbled across the dusty Serengeti with the setting sun at our backs. My thoughts tumbled willy-nilly around the three things I will always remember about that trip. The Serengeti itself, trapping the past in a vast sponge of trackless wilderness. An American who was still so close to his own culture that he had not yet adapted to ours in Africa. And a naive yet lovable young African who had been studying English alone for nine years in the middle of nowhere, and who thought America was rich because everyone there was Christian.

"The endless, open plains create an aura of serenity."

10/Danieli Makala

There was a certain familiarity to the scene, figures in a tableau that I had seen before, frozen into immobility by the softly modulated voice of the pastor praying for the patient. But there was something different about it also, and for the moment the reason eluded me.

The patient, due to enter the hospital for surgery the next day, sat on the edge of a low meninga-wood chair in the corner of my living room. She sat upright, head bowed, hands loosely clasped in her lap, eyes closed, completely relaxed as she listened to the smooth flow of perfect idiomatic Swahili. She was not seriously ill, nor was the operation to be a big one, but there was a degree of anxiety commensurate with the anticipation of the general anesthetic and surgical procedure, and I knew that there was comfort for this deeply religious woman in the prayers for her safety and well-being.

The pastor sat forward on the edge of his chair, elbows on knees, his fingers touching gracefully at their tips, his head bowed and eyes closed, the classic portrait of a man of God talking to his God. The prayer was not long, perhaps no more than four or five minutes, a supplication to God to be with the patient, to augment her strength, to protect her from harm, to bring her out of the hospital whole and well again. Then the pastor thanked God that this patient was what she was, a nurse who had helped to save the lives and preserve the health of thousands of people. It was then I fully realized what there was about this little scene that was different, although an awareness had been flitting on the edge of conscious thought for some time.

You see, the woman listening to the prayers was a white missionary and the man praying was a black pastor. The bread cast upon the waters had returned. The wheel had come full circle. And the interesting thing was that it all seemed so natural, taking a bit of thought to even notice it. I'm quite sure that neither the pastor nor the patient thought there was anything strange about the situation, but I had only been in Africa for about 2½ years and was still able to perceive the significance of the scene.

The black man's name was Danieli Makala. He was my pastor also, and I have listened to him preach dozens of times, and he has been in my home often. In some ways he was not exceptional, and in others he was.

He was an Iramba man, born and raised in the rolling bushland atop the plateau on which most of his tribesmen live. His childhood home was a mud-brick house with a flat mud roof which grew a lush green carpet of grass during the rainy season. At the end of the rains he often climbed with his mother to the roof to work with the millet and the corn, preparing it for grinding into the meal which would be breakfast and supper for the next year.

From the roof he could see the courtyard surrounded

by the other houses in their *boma,* and by a tall hedge of poles, most of which had taken root and had begun to sprout leaves and to grow again. They formed a living corral in which the cattle and sheep and goats could be held safely at night, protecting them from leopards, hyenas and people. Before he started to school he went each morning from this home to shepherd the animals to grass and water, sometimes alone and sometimes with his sister. Sometimes his sister went alone, and on one of these occasions she met a lion in the path, and conquered fear, an incident Danieli used in a sermon I heard when he was no longer just Danieli, but Pastor Makala.

I wish I had known his parents when they were younger, because to produce a son like Danieli Makala they must have been truly inspiring people. When I knew the father he was already aged, somewhat senile, walking the lanes and roads aimlessly, *kichaa* (not quite right mentally). But in his manhood he must have been strong of mind and of spirit, for he was a first-generation Christian at a time when it was not easy. I never knew Pastor Makala's mother, but she must have been a real lady, teaching Danieli the gentle and proper manners of a well-brought-up Iramba boy. For in Danieli Makala there is a most interesting blending of strength of purpose, force of will, gentleness of spirit, and deep understanding of the meaning of the human soul and its relationship to God.

Danieli Makala went to a Lutheran Mission grade school, several miles from his home, and he walked or ran back and forth each day. In the Iramba-land of that day, not really so many years ago, more children tended the cattle than went to school, for schools still were not common, and school fees were hard to find. But Danieli finished grade school, then went to middle school, which brought his level of education up to that of freshman or sophomore in high school in America. Seminary training was next, at Makumira, near Arusha, a tree-shaded campus of just two or three buildings. From there Danieli Makala emerged with his degree as a pastor.

It is interesting to note in passing that the Swahili word for pastor is "*mchungaji*," or "shepherd," the same word that is applied to the herdsmen who guard their cattle from wild animals and who lead them to water and to fresh green grass. "*Mchungaji*" is in turn derived from the verb "*kuchunga*," which means literally "to protect," or "to guard." Danieli Makala became a protector, a guardian. Protector of the faith; guardian of the children of God.

I first met Danieli Makala in 1963 when he came to Kiomboi Hospital as chaplain to the patients. From a distance he was not an impressive figure, did not stand out in a crowd. Of normal height for an Iramba man, with close-cropped black hair, chocolate-brown skin rather than black, of sturdy but lean build, dressed in Western clothes, he was not one you would notice above many others. But immediately when you met him, you *felt* the difference, perhaps undefinable at first, but you could sense it.

Danieli is different. It's in his eyes, his face, the lines of his jaw, the modulation of his voice, the smile on his lips. It's in the way he greets you; he makes you feel bigger and better. He does this to you. Without trying, without knowing it, he radiates warmth and friendliness. A man who loves. A man to be loved.

It has been many years since a missionary has been *mchungaji* to the Kiomboi Church, so Danieli Makala was our preacher, teacher, and counselor. Kiomboi has one of the oldest congregations in Iramba-land, founded in the '30s, now numbering almost a thousand Christians if one counts the tiny bush churches which it has "mothered" over the years, and which send their members into the main church for services from time to time. *Mchungaji* Makala was indeed our shepherd. He performed the rites and the sacraments of the church — baptism, marriage, communion, confirmation. He talked to the patients at the hospital and visited the sick in their homes. I shall tell you a story in a moment about a visit to a dying man in his house on the Zalala River.

Pastor Makala's assistant was an uneducated man who was called an "evangelist," according to local terminology. This was a euphemism which meant he was a man who felt called by the vocation of the ministry, but who had not had the advantage of formal schooling beyond the knowledge of reading and writing. We called him *mchungaji,* too — Mchungaji Masisala — and he *was* a shepherd. Earnest, sincere, devout, he preached in the big church about once a month. He chose a different text each time, but his theological training was too limited to allow him to preach many different sermons. But he spoke from the heart, and he knew the Bible, and he spoke to us of his own experiences in life. He once preached an entire sermon of thanks to God for saving his life after he had been bitten by a poisonous snake. (He was right, of course, for I saw the tooth-marks in his foot, and the swelling didn't go down for almost two weeks, low on the side of the foot near the little toe. From the position of the fang-marks, I suspected that he had been bitten by an adder, a pit-viper, since they cannot rise up to strike like the cobra or the mamba.) He was a big man, tall and straight and muscular, with a powerful face. When I first knew him, Mr. Masisala wore a long white gown which reached the ground, and he was often barefoot when he wasn't in church, but in later years he wore the more convenient trousers, white shirt and shoes of the more affluent (or Westernized) Africans.

Pastor Makala was one of the few Africans with whom I really felt comfortable. I have thought about this many times. In the almost three years that I lived on the Iramba Plateau, I came to know a great number of Africans fairly well. Pastors, teachers, nurses, policemen, government officials and workers, farmers, men and women in all walks of life. I felt at home with Eliasafi Ndemsumburo, our chief maintenance man, and with Nehemiah Yakobo, our senior medical assistant, and with Police Commander Mazwile at New Kiomboi. But there was oftentimes a constraint, a lack of full communication, with most of the others I knew. They would come into our home, and we would go into theirs, and we would talk for a few moments about odds and ends, and then there would be the barrier. We were of different worlds, of alien cultures; our goals and aims were superficially the same but actually disparate. It was not a matter of black and white, of African and American, of doctor and teacher (or nurse, farmer, or mechanic), although those were contributing factors. No, it went deeper than that. We each lacked the ability to *comprehend* what the other was as a person, what made us what we were, what "made us tick." I fail to find better words to describe the dilemma we faced than to say that we just didn't understand each other.

But I think that Danieli Makala and I understood each other. Or to put it another way: we found enough common ground under our feet so that we could talk about our problems and ideas. We had common interests.

Oh, there were areas in his life which I would never penetrate, and there were parts of my life and thought which I could never hope to communicate to him. After all, we both were tied to our cultures; as much as we might want to cut some of those ties to better understand the other, it was impossible.

But he gave me insights into his life and character, and presumably I reciprocated. If anything, I would suspect that he "read" me better than I did him, because, for one thing, he was very astute and perceptive, and for another, I think a person acting within his own culture, as Pastor Makala naturally did, does not stand out in such bold relief as one who acts in his normal way in a totally foreign culture, such as I did.

As one continues to live month after month (and then year after year) in a foreign culture, he gradually begins at least to see the reason for a thing being done the way it is, even if he can never quite understand it. But it is one thing to watch something happening, perhaps even understanding it, and yet another to merge one's own personality and attitudes into that happening in such a way as to be inconspicuous. For example, I could never go to a wedding in Irambaland and enter unhesitatingly and spontaneously into the dancing and singing. It was *too* unlike our weddings at home. Furthermore, I was not expected to lose my identity, nor could I change my color. I was an outsider, welcome but apart.

Slowly, however, after I had attended several weddings, and had the various occurrences explained to me, they no longer seemed odd or strange. But even after the people and their customs no longer seemed strange, *I* still did not fit in any better than I had at first. I noted, too, that even Americans who had been in Africa for twenty years did not ever *really* identify with Africans in events which were typically African. It was impossible. Only if an American child were to grow up in an African house, eat African food, go to an African school, fear the African nights and be treated by an African medicine man or witch-doctor, could he ever hope to empathize completely with the African.

This doesn't mean that one shouldn't try! An American will be forgiven many errors if his *attitudes* are right, and one of the attitudes he must have is that the African has within him (and within his culture) ideas and customs and mores that are worthy of emulation and respect. If he does not have this attitude, he will be useless, or worse yet, do actual harm to his cause. The African will forgive him without blinking an eyelash for saying "*Sitaki*" instead of "*Sipendi*" when he is offered more food, but he will never forget it if the foreigner insists that "*Sitaki*" is really *better* than "*Sipendi.*"

So, in general, I repeat, the strangeness of African ways gradually loses its strangeness, but the American never does, no matter how hard he tries. And he can try too hard. It was Pastor Makala who pointed this out to me, and I will never forget what he said. We were talking about a tall young Englishman, Patrick Pender-Cudlipp, who was living with Africans while studying their dialect, customs, history and folkstories. He had identified as well with the local people as anyone I have ever seen. But Pastor Makala said, "That's very well for him, because he is trying to learn, not to teach. He is young and adjusts quickly and easily to a new kind of life. And when he goes home he will quickly readjust to his former life.* But an older person who has come out for a short period of time, who has come to teach us something we don't know, such as a doctor or pastor or teacher, reduces his effectiveness if he has to spend too much time doing the many things necessary just to stay alive and healthy in an African type of life. He must live a life which is as normal for him as it can be, and then he will have the time, and the energy, and the desire to perform as he should."

But even as I write this, I can remember many incidents which seemed strange, and which I never did fully understand. There was the laughter — true laughter, not the embarrassed kind — when the death of someone was announced to an African. There was the pervading sense of evil in the beauty of the black night. There was the unimaginative fatalism of the tribal African when confronted with danger or sickness or storms. There was the rigid, unyielding grip of clan and tribe which stifled initiative and perhaps partly

* Africans dubbed Patrick "*Bwana Mmoja na Nusu,*" Mr. One and a Half, because he was about 6′ 6″ tall.

explains the total lack of development of tribal societies until an external stimulus is applied.

On a more superficial plane, there were other things that seemed strange even after a couple of years in Irambaland, incidents that demonstrate the differences between our cultures. Many of them are scattered through this book, but one involving Pastor Makala should be recorded here.

Early one morning I was preparing to make a business trip to Singida, sixty miles away, by Land-Rover. Since our trips were so infrequent, we tried to accomplish as much as we could on each safari. My wife Edna was going in to do some shopping for us and a half-dozen other people, Pastor Makala was going to a synod meeting, and Godson Makala (no relation to the pastor) was going along since he had never been to the big city.

At the last moment I found I had to help move one of our mechanics, Zakaria, who was being transferred to Singida. We stopped at his house, and I waited for him to get out and get his belongings. But he remained seated and before I knew what was happening, Pastor Makala had jumped out of the Land-Rover to get Zakaria's things from the house, had climbed up on the car, and was lashing down the gear. Zakaria still sat there. Against my better judgment I got out also and climbed up on the car and helped the pastor. Both he and I were twice the age of Zakaria, and there he sat in the car while we sweated in the hot sun lashing down his gear. It slowly dawned on me that this had to be some local custom, and indeed it was. A person going on a journey does little himself to prepare for the journey and Pastor Makala was acting out this custom.

Zakaria was nonchalant, unconcerned that his pastor was up on the top of the car tying down the chair and rugs. Not a word was said at the time; the deed was just done, as odd as it seemed to me. To fully appreciate the oddity, one only needs to translate this episode to a small town in the United States. It just couldn't happen! This is just one relatively minor incident, one of hundreds (thousands?) that occurred in the three years I lived there. One feels his way along, trying not to offend, watching others and copying as closely as possible, and hoping for the forgiveness of ignorance.

Despite these myriad differences, Danieli Makala and I found a rapport with each other which transcended racial and cultural dissimilarities. Was he black and I white? I don't remember. Was his first language Swahili and mine English? I don't recall. Had he skipped high school and I had gone much further? I forget. Did he eat *uji* for breakfast and I cornflakes? It was unimportant. *Was he a man? Ndio. Kweli.* (It is so. Truly.)

It is always difficult to characterize a man in one word and perhaps one shouldn't try, but there is a word that leaps to the mind when one considers Danieli Makala: Compassionate. You could see it in the look he gave the sick, in the smile that hovered on his lips and in his eyes when he spoke to a beggar-man. You could hear it in his voice when he handed the cup to the communicant at the altar.

I'll never forget the time I went with him to visit a dying man just a mile or so from Kiomboi. There were four of us, Pastor Makala, his wife, Eric, and myself. It was late at night as we drove down the hard-packed dirt road from the hospital, the headlights picking up the glaring red eyes of hyenas in the fields and glinting off the water standing in the swamp by the water pump. The road gave out and we followed a winding footpath through the cornfields, almost to the banks of the Zalala River. It was absolutely pitch dark when we turned off the ignition and the headlights and set out single-file on a narrow path, the corn high above our heads on either side, making a tunnel through the blackness. We stopped at one house, found no one home, and pushed on. We stumbled over a ridge of earth which once had been a house, now worn down by torrents of rain and wind, and found ourselves in the dark courtyard of a house. Just outside the door were two women and a child holding their hands over a few glowing coals which threw off a little heat but no light. Pastor Makala called out "*Hodi*," and we heard the answer from inside, "*Karibuni*."

Inside the house there was a faint light from a small kerosene flame placed on the five-foot-high mudbrick divider between the main room and the sleeping room to the left. There was no furniture. An old, old woman sat with her back to the divider, her legs straight out in front of her in characteristic fashion. Another form lay on a cowskin, completely covered with a blanket; this person never moved during the hour we were there.

Against the opposite wall sat a middle-aged man, his face haggard in the flickering light. His knees were drawn up against his chest, his coal-black robe drawn down over his feet completely covering his body, and leaning back against his legs was an old man sitting in exactly the same position with a similar black robe covering his body. They were two mounds of blackness, with ebony faces etched deeply with sorrow. Pastor and Mrs. Makala immediately went through the room into a third room on the right and we could hear an exchange of greetings in the local dialect. Eric and I stayed in the main room, and were offered split logs to sit on.

An old man was dying of tuberculosis. He had been seen in the hospital, and had been treated, but it was too late and he was dying. He was a Christian and before he lost consciousness he wanted the Pastor to come to him, and pray with him. His wife was with him. There was small talk for ten or fifteen minutes, then silence, and then the pastor began to pray. His voice was low, almost a whisper, but the quietness of the night was so profound that we could hear every word. The old lady across from me sat with bowed head and closed eyes. The two men sitting tandem on my right disappeared into the shadows of their robes. The single flame from the lamp flickered in the gloom. Eric sat unmoving and still, in awesome reverence of death and God in the same house.

The pastor concluded his prayer, and his wife picked it up, musically, as if in antiphony, and the mesmerization continued. *God,* I thought, *O God, has anyone ever died in such peace?* I remember thinking then, although it sounds somewhat silly now (or does it?) that when I died I would like to hear those same two voices praying for me, in Kinylamba, in words that only God could understand, for when we pray do we pray so that men can hear us or so that God will hear? The voice stopped. *Amin.*

Again there was silence. A beetle dived at the lamp and rattled on the mud divider and then was still. There was a faint soughing of the wind in the corn outside. The child was asleep by the fire. Across from me the old woman stirred, then broke the silence with a single word, "*Songela*" (Thank you). Then she began to pray, her voice husky with emotion, the words coming hesitatingly and quietly at first, then growing stronger and more melodious until she was almost singing, the words rolling, lilting, honey-soft, in a language made for song, with no r's or gutturals, no z's or hard g's, no flat a's, no nasals or twanging sounds. And then she was through. *Amin.*

Absolute silence. No mosquitoes or flies to irritate. Complete peace. I looked out through the open door and could see the stars shining in the heavens. Wood smoke and kerosene smoke mixed not unpleasantly in the small room. It was time to go, and I could hear the pastor and his wife saying good-by in the next room, and soon we were outside in the darkness again, tunneling through the cornfield to the car.

The old man died during the night, and surely no man has ever left this life in closer harmony with man and God.

This was Danieli Makala's life, to bring peace and harmony to Kiomboi. How well did he succeed? Who can tell? His success will not be measured in the numbers of East African shillings in the offering plate each Sunday, nor in the yearly increase in the standard of living of the African farmer, nor can you measure "goodwill" engendered between people of different classes, religions, races. But my judgment is that he succeeded very well, for even though you can't measure the effects of his ministry, you can see it. I know, for I was there and he was a good shepherd.

Rev. Makala was pastor of the Kiomboi church.

11/Ramadhani Kamata

I'm not sure that I ever really liked Ramadhani Kamata. I'm pretty sure he didn't like me. I was American, white, educated, "rich," impatient, Christian. He was African, black, uneducated, "poor," patient, Muslim.* He spoke not a word of English and I not a word of Kinyaturu, but we both spoke Swahili. And we both spoke the language of the hunter. Where it counted in our relationship we could communicate with each other on a plane deeper than that of mere language. So it was there, that odd bond between two disparate entities: I needed him, and he needed me. I never went hunting in his territory without stopping to pick up him and his son, and he always went with me, except one time when he was too busy with his gum-collecting business, and even on that occasion I asked him to hand-pick one of his men to go with us. (I was not real happy with his choice!)

* I have put "rich" and "poor" in quotes because I was poor by my standards, living on a missionary's salary, but rich by his; and he was very well-off by African standards, but poor by mine.

Ramadhani Kamata was a rather short man for a Turu. Perhaps he had some Iramba blood in him, for most Turus are tall, and the Irambas are short. Lately there have been more and more frequent inter-tribal marriages, because their boundaries meet where the western edge of the Iramba Plateau drops off onto the Wembere Plains, the traditional home of the Wataturu. His face was strong, full of character, black because he was a Bantu, and blacker still because he lived out of doors in a latitude where the sun's rays do not angulate through layers of atmosphere and smoke and fog.

His nose was prominent, his lips slightly everted, but even so the over-all effect of his face was one of angles and planes, perhaps because his cheekbones were high, almost Mongoloid, and his chin chiseled and sharply molded. His eyes were black, or so dark brown that they looked black, and bitingly clear and penetrating. Maybe this was why I sometimes felt uncomfortable with him: I had the feeling he could look into me and know me, but I could never hope to know him. I'll never forget the look he gave me when I took a wild, desperate shot at a fleeing wildebeest instead of stalking it until I could get a good clean kill.

"Bwana," those eyes said, "you've never done that before and I hope you never do it again. It was not worthy of a true hunter."

He was right of course, and that hurt. For two hours we drove hard and tracked harder, and eventually got the animal, and in an adolescent attempt to regain his respect, I gave him the entire 'beest. But I don't think even that was enough.

He dressed as many of the more affluent tribesmen have begun to do, in a pair of rather dirty shorts and an even dirtier T-shirt, with a short jacket that once was blue and had a zipper that worked. On his belt he carried a crude knife with a short triangular blade that he kept sharp by honing it on any convenient rock or my whetstone when I was with him. In addition, he never went far from camp without his two-foot *panga,* a broad-bladed machete. I never saw him with spear or bow and arrow; perhaps he felt he had gone beyond that stage, for most of his fellow tribesmen carried one or the other, sometimes both.

Ramadhani lived about halfway down the ten-mile-long slope from the Iramba Plateau to the Wembere Plains. His home was typical of the Wataturu, a long, low mud house that was raftered strongly with saplings, and which was part of the wall that surrounded a holding pen for the cattle. This *boma* enclosed a plot of ground about a half acre in size. I think the houses in Ramadhani's *boma* must have housed 25-50 people, for whenever I stopped at his home, I was greeted immediately by an outpouring of men and women of all ages. A half-dozen small children stood silently by their mothers, eyes wide and alert, senses sharpened for flight if necessary. The mothers were frankly curious, and those who could speak Swahili immediately engaged me in conversation.

Once I was startled when a young woman standing back in the crowd piped up with "Good morning," in English, and I answered her slowly and distinctly, "Good morning, how are you?" (It was about 8 P.M.). She answered, "Fine, thank you." I tried a few more sentences in English, and that was the extent of the English conversation. We talked further in Swahili and I found that she had gone to our own Lutheran Girls' School at Ruruma for enough years to learn a little English, but that had been some years before and she had forgotten most of it.

Once a roly-poly little fellow ran up to me, then fell grotesquely in an epileptic fit. No one moved to help him so I bent to pull his teeth out of his tongue. Looking around at the group, I saw they were studiously ignoring the youngster. I knew they assumed him to be bewitched, and therefore they could do nothing for him lest they themselves fall under the spell. Only ten miles away was Ushora dispensary where they could have received a free supply of drugs to prevent or modify the attacks. I reminded them of this. They were unimpressed.

After we picked up Ramadhani and his son Athumani, we finished the descent from the plateau through dense forest, on a sand track that snaked through the trees and underbrush. This particular part of Tanzania always reminded me of the tote roads and fire lanes in northwestern Wisconsin, except of course that the trees were of a different kind. But it was reminiscent and I always remarked on it when my family was along – like a broken record, I'm told – every time we ground down the slope. I was rewarded with a patient "Yes, dear," from my wife, or a "Yeah, Dad," from Eric, or a slightly more sympathetic, "Yes, Daddy," from Barbara.

When the road flattened out on the Wembere Plains it straightened a little, still following ancient footpaths, across a deep and muddy river, through dry swamps where elephants had walked in the rainy season and left deep holes through which we literally had to crawl with the Land-Rover. Half an hour later we arrived at the *gundi* camp, Mduguyu, where temporary grass lean-tos were constructed during the dry season to shelter the two hundred men who came from all over the plains to gather thorn-tree sap for the production of gum-arabic. Ramadhani supervised the collection of the gum, but it didn't keep him from hunting with me except for the one time I really wanted him because I had the Ray Larsons visiting us from our home in Wisconsin. From Mduguyu it was just a short ten minute drive into the completely uninhabited bush country where we set up camp and hunted.

Ramadhani always sat on my left, in the middle of the seat, so he could see ahead and to both sides. My other hunting partner, usually my thirteen-year-old son Eric, sat on the far left, and everyone else sat in back. We almost always had three or four other people –

other missionaries, African personnel from the hospital, Ramadhani's son, visitors from other parts of Africa or from the States. But Ramadhani was my guide and tracker. He was my eyes and my compass. He had been born and raised in that bush and was never lost. We could drive in circles for hours, looking for game, shooting game, following wounded animals, and I would not pay the slightest heed to where we were, or where we were going, for I knew that when we were ready to go back to camp Ramadhani would get us there by the shortest route. I learned the country, too, of course, and after a few months could not have become "permanently" lost, but often would have taken the long way to camp.

Ramadhani didn't like to sit outside on the hood or the overhead rack. Eric often did when we were hunting birds for the pot, and once he and Godson Makala, our young gardener, were sitting up on top of the Land-Rover when they spotted a pride of lions; I stopped the car immediately so they could get inside. I remember that incident with disgust and I still feel that Ramadhani failed me completely. It was not all his fault; maybe not even half his fault, but I was provoked. We followed the lions for a quarter of a mile or so, through very dense bush and tall yellow elephant grass. We had seen a young female, and an older female with three or four tiny cubs, and then suddenly Ramadhani saw a third big lion off to the left about 200 yards, streaking through the grass, apparently trying to cross in front of us to join the female with the cubs.

"*Dume, bwana, dume mkubwa sana!!*" Ramadhani yelled excitedly. (A male, sir, a very big male.)

I had not been able to identify the lion as a male, and he didn't have much of a mane, no more than the usual neck hair that even a big female will have. But he was big, and I angled the Land-Rover toward him. He stayed even with us, then stopped when he saw he could not get across in front of us. I stopped, too; he was not more than a hundred yards away, perhaps less.

"Ramadhani," I asked, "are you sure it's a male?"

"Yes, indeed," he answered, "no question about it."

A second African in back concurred. Excited about the prospect of filling my lion license, I jumped out of the Land-Rover, and just as the lion decided to run off, I put a 220 grain silvertip through its shoulder. It ran about fifty yards and dropped down dead.

We drove over to it and when I looked at it I was almost physically ill. A lioness. Dead. An illegal trophy.

Angrily I asked Ramadhani how he had been so sure it was a male. He shrugged and said, "*Ukubwa tu.*" (Just the size.)

Your guess is as good as mine as to what his motives were in urging me to shoot with such a flimsy identification. Did he really think it was a male, or did he just want the lion killed? We were only a half mile from our tent camp, and only about two miles from his *gundi* camp, and lions can roam miles in a night. But there are lions around all the time. We had heard this pride earlier in the morning before daybreak as we were heating up our coffee on the remnants of last night's coals. Even though it was, in the end, my own fault and responsibility for the killing, I have always sort of blamed Ramadhani whether he deserved it or not.

I got over my little fit of pique and we went back to camp for breakfast. He knew I was irritated, however, and he got even with me later. When we were ready to go home, I said, "I'd like to leave off some meat at the *gundi* camp for some other friends of mine."

"All right," he said, "let's cut through this part of the bush and we'll come out on the track further on down."

I argued with him for a moment, feeling it would be better to start right out on the track from camp even if it were a longer drive. He was as stubborn as a Scotchman, and won out. We took the shortcut, over some of the roughest, most potholed, elephant-tracked bush that I have ever been in. Before we were halfway across I was mumbling under my breath about how stupid I was, and not long after I was mumbling out loud how stupid *he* was, and I was just about to lose my temper completely when we broke out of the bush onto the track to the *gundi* camp. Ramadhani had a supercilious grin on his face, and I couldn't help laughing in spite of myself. Okay, you win, I thought to myself. It *had* been a shorter trip, in distance, but not in time.

But despite our occasional irritation with each other, we worked well as a team. I never failed to take his advice about where to look for a particular species of animal that I wanted to get. When I wanted eland, he showed them to me. If it was zebra, he took me to them. Wildebeest? Let's go this way, *bwana*. I drove the Land-Rover, paid for the petrol, carried the rifle, and shot the game. I was about ten percent of the team; he was the other ninety percent.

Oh, I've gone hunting without a guide and tracker, and I've come home with meat, but it took longer to find the game, and I had to stay alert as to where I was, and couldn't really get too far from the track that would take me out. And if I wounded an animal, it took much longer to find it again. With Ramadhani I lost only one wounded animal, a wildebeest that I had hit well and was certain would die. He told his friends in the *gundi* camp about the animal, and they continued tracking it the next day, and found it, dead.

One of the annoying aspects of our hunting partnership stemmed from the fact that Ramadhani was a Muslim. A Muslim will never eat pork, nor will he eat the meat of any animal that has not been ritually killed. A Muslim, or a Christian pastor, must cut the throat of the animal before it dies, and say a few prescribed words. This custom made things inconvenient in a number of ways. For one thing, Ramadhani was always in an extreme hurry to get to a kill before the animal had drawn its last breath so that he could "kill" it ceremoniously and therefore be able to eat the meat. The knife was drawn across the neck, almost severing the head, care being taken to cut both carotids and jugulars, as well as the trachea. The part I especially didn't like was loading that bloody carcass in the Land-Rover, particularly if we were on a hunt of more than one day, because the blood attracted flies and there was never enough water to clean out the car.

But it was even more troublesome when once or twice each trip we didn't get to the animal in time for the ritual throat-cutting. Ramadhani wasn't angry when this happened; he was just uncooperative. There apparently is a religious taboo about even touching "unclean" meat. If it was a small animal, like a Tommy or an impala, he merely sat off to the side while we took care of the animal, usually just a matter of loading it into the Land-Rover to take back to camp where we would clean it and salt the skin.

If it was a bigger animal like a wildebeest, *kongoni*, eland or zebra, Ramadhani would reluctantly help us. A real problem arose if we already had a "clean" animal in the Land-Rover, because the unclean animal could not come in contact with it or it too would become unclean. Then we would have to load the unclean animal on top of the Land-Rover, and if it was a big one it was very difficult. If the animal inside the Land-Rover was small and had not dripped blood on the floor, we could throw it up on top and load the other one inside. But if there was blood on the floor, we couldn't even do that. We were always able to figure out some way to handle things, but it was a bloody nuisance!

Ramadhani loved to have his picture taken with any animal worthy of a picture. Most of the more unsophisticated Africans do like to get into pictures, and they are overjoyed when you get a print made and give it to them. Most of the time I took Kodachromes, but on one trip I took some black and white pictures and promised to get Ramadhani a print. It took about three months to get the pictures back, return the negative to England for reproduction, and then remember to take the picture with me when I went hunting. Each time I arrived at Ramadhani's *boma,* the first thing he would say was, "Where's the picture?" Finally one day I did remember to take it with me, and when I showed it to him he stared at it until he was nearly mesmerized. Excitedly he showed it to his friends around the *gundi* camp and it was a half hour before I could get Ramadhani and his picture back into the Land-Rover. It was worth the effort and the expense to see the happiness that the picture brought him, and Ramadhani was exceptionally eager to please me on that trip. I don't think we crossed swords more than two or three times the whole weekend!

I never ceased to be amazed at the ease with which Ramadhani could just take off for two or three days and hunt with me, without having had any notice that I was coming. I had to plan each hunt weeks in advance, making sure I could rent the station Land-Rover, checking with Dr. Rude about any important plans which would take him away from the station, lining up the other members of the party, and so forth. But when we arrived, unannounced, at Ramadhani's *boma,* I would say, "Hello, Ramadhani, we're going hunting for the next two days."

"Yes," he would say, "I see you are."

"Can you go with us?"

"Certainly, just wait until I get my shoes and my blanket."

And that was that. This happened every time except when the Larsons came. One time we chanced to meet him on the road down to the Wembere Plains from Urugu; he just got into the Land-Rover with his son, drove with us to his *boma* to get his shoes and his blanket, and off we went. Either he didn't have anything else to do, or getting meat was always more important. I never deluded myself that he liked me so much that he was always willing to drop everything to go with me! I have already indicated that I'm not sure he even liked me at all. But he always went.

This was generally true of most of the Africans whom I knew away from the hospital compound. They had little or nothing to do, and whatever they might have to do could easily be put off for a day or two, or a week or two. *Si haraka, bwana.* (There's no hurry, sir.) Or, *haraka, haraka, haina baraka.* (Hurrying, hurrying, brings no blessings – their version of "haste makes waste.")

I have no quarrel whatsoever with this attitude, this part of their culture. It works well for them when they stay within their culture. But one runs into troubles when the African moves out of his culture into a situation where there must be modification of his traditional habits. One hears and reads so much about the attempts of the white man to "westernize" the African against his better judgment and opposed to his own culture and welfare. I will not argue with this on any grounds other than the one I know best by personal experience, and that is in the field of health care. I am completely and thoroughly convinced that it is absolutely necessary to "westernize" the African to make him a good doctor, medical assistant, nurse, or technician. Why? Because until every patient becomes a challenge, he will not do his best. Until every problem becomes a bee in his bonnet, until he cannot rest until the answer is found, he will not be a good health worker. Until punctuality becomes important, until overtime becomes unimportant, until efficiency becomes second-nature, he will be a second-rate health worker.

He must initiate actions, he must think for himself, he must consider alternatives and choose the best, he must offer suggestions – all these things he must do on his own, and these are the very things he does not by nature do. Only when he becomes "westernized" does he begin to function as a worthwhile addition to the medical team, rather than just another body who can perform routine tasks when told exactly what to do. Most Africans are afraid to strike out alone on an idea of their own, without prior consultation with others. This is an old custom, and works well in tribal life, but in the hospital it is an undesirable trait. The motto, "do it yourself," could well be changed to "think for yourself."

Someone is bound to ask a certain question about Ramadhani Kamata; I know this because I have talked about him to a number of different people and have shown pictures of him to friends. The question goes something like this, "Well, he was sort of the 'noble savage' type, wasn't he?"

To me, this is an irritating question. He was, of course, noble. He was clean cut, honest, devout (in his own way), and he certainly had a confident attitude about him which always said louder than words that he was no one's inferior. In fact, I had the distinct feeling that he thought I was the inferior. And I was, when I was in his country. I couldn't see as far nor as sharply. I couldn't walk or run as far nor as fast. I needed to use sunglasses or my eyes would be burning red by evening from sun and dust. I couldn't go to bed at night without washing my hands and face. I was always drinking water. At night I used a canvas cot, two blankets, and whenever I could take it, a pillow. I was squeamish about digging my hands into an animal's belly when the guts were ruptured (I *did do* it, but only if I could think of no intellectually honest way to get someone else to do it.) I did not know the bush, nor where the waterholes were. I could not sleep at night if the mosquitoes were biting me. I was not a man, in the sense that he was a man.

So in this context, he was "noble." I would not say he was not. And of course, he was not a savage, at least not in the dictionary definition of the word, which implies a human being living somewhat like an animal, in an uncivilized, primitive way.* I have made the point time and again, when speaking to groups or in casual conversation with the neighbors, that we must *never* use the term uncivilized when talking about the Africans I have known. I will go so far as to say that their civilization is different from ours, but I will quickly add that it is a very distinct civilization nevertheless. White men have not taken the time to investigate this culture, or if they have, most still have failed to grasp its significance. I will even insist that the nomadic Bushmen in the Kindira Mountains near Kiomboi, close relatives to the Bushmen of the Kalahari, have a civilization. It is not one we can identify with, nor one we would want to be part of, but it *is* a civilization. We are too prone to say, yes, *we* are civilized, and any cultural pattern that does not meet our standards is an inferior type of culture, *ergo*, it is *not* civilized. Do you think I am being romantic and semantic? I do not.

I am not sure just what I expected of Ramadhani Kamata when I told him I would not be returning to Mduguyu again. Would he grip my hand in farewell and tell me how much he had enjoyed our hunts together? Would he reminisce about all the game we had taken, and the dangers we had laughed at, the mosquitoes we had swatted, the female lion he had insisted I shoot? Would he mention the campfires we had sat around in the darkness of the African night listening to the hunting roars of the lions and the weird calls of the prowling hyenas and the guttural coughs of the leopards? Just what would he say?

I am glad I did not anticipate any melodramatic

* *Webster's New World Dictionary.*

ending to our odysseys in the bush and grasslands of the Wembere Plains, for he said as he shook my hand, "Will another doctor come to take your place at Kiomboi, and will he come down here to hunt?" The perfect squelch.

A typical, if not ego-gratifying, response, for the African is above all else a pragmatist. "If you do not come to hunt anymore, who will? I have burned my *gundi* village and shall not rebuild it for six months, and will have nothing to do except hunt during that time, and now you say you are leaving. Who will come to take your place?" All this was implied in his question.

Indeed, who will?

"Ramadhani Kamata (kneeling) was my guide and tracker . . . my eyes and my compass."

12 / Yonatani

He was not the least recalcitrant. When he was asked why he wrote such a thing on the professor's blackboard he said, "I don't really know. It just came to me, so I did it. And I'm not the least bit sorry. I meant it then and I mean it now. The white man has got to realize he's just here for a short time more."

Yonitani was an average college student, which meant that he was superior in every measurable way to his age peers around the rest of the country. He was quiet, short of stature (about 5′1″), with fiery eyes that the professor later described as "demonic," yet he was a hard worker and a brilliant scholar. His beginnings had been humble enough but gradually over the years he had pulled away from his people and the village in which he had been raised. He was born in a small mud and wattle hut, his aunt attending the birth, and he spent his pre-school years playing in the courtyard of the circle of houses in which his family and his relatives lived.

At the age of eight he started in Standard One at

the Mission School two miles away, and the years flew by. He began learning Swahili in the first grade and English in the fourth. By the time he had finished Sixth Standard he could use Swahili as well as his own tribal dialect, and was able to make himself understood in English. Selected to go on to Middle School (equivalent to grades seven and eight) on the basis of examinations, he began to sense his superiority to the others who went back to the farm. Middle School was easy for him, and he came out on top in every subject, paving the way for Secondary School. His high marks, together with strong recommendations from his teacher, pastor, and the sub-chief of his tribe, made him one of the very few young men eligible for Secondary School.

Insidiously the feeling of being one of the elite crept into his consciousness. His Swahili was flawless, his English excellent. In conversations with Europeans and Americans he always swung over into English to demonstrate his ability, telling himself that he was just practicing, but deep in his heart he knew he was showing off. He always wore a white shirt, usually with a tie, and at home he refused to work in the fields any more.

Secondary School was 200 miles away, in Arusha, so he got home only once every three to four months. This suited him fine, for what could he do in the tiny village where he was born? It was more fun to go into the town where he could see movies from England and America or sit with his friends in the beer hall and spend a pleasant evening in that way. He studied hard also, preparing for the university which he craved more and more as his birthright. Classes were all in English and his ability to handle the language grew rapidly. He began reading newspapers in English rather than Swahili and found a whole new world opening to him.

He didn't realize it then, but he was developing what would later be derisively called the "colonial mentality." At his young age, he could not really remember the struggle for independence, nor could he remember, even by trying hard, the effects of colonialism on his village or his school. So for long years he scarcely understood what he read in the papers about the brutality of the British, the submerging of the African culture, the demeaning of the African personality, the attempt by the colonialists to pervert the African mind, the insidious spiriting away of the riches of Africa to a foreign country. His only contact with the *Wazungu* (white people) was with the missionaries at home and his teachers at Secondary School, and they had been, for the most part, helpful, courteous, and above all, rich. The *Wazungu* were the ones with the good clothes, sturdy shoes, nice homes, radios, automobiles, and so many other personal belongings that they were to be envied, not hated, as long as one was on the way up to such a status himself. And there was no question in his mind that these *Wazungu* were the possessors of all this wealth because they were *educated,* and this was to be his heritage.

Inevitably he went on to "higher school," two years of schooling equivalent to junior college in the States. He was still isolated from the world around him, still quite untouched by the furor now resounding in the country about independence, nationalism, socialism, self-reliance. Still he was fettered, according to his later reminiscences about that time of his life, by the colonial mentality. His primary aim was to get an education, and he never once thought that he didn't deserve what he was getting.

He saw no reason for washing his own clothes, cleaning his room, raking the schoolgrounds, sweeping the floors. After all, there were well-paid servants to do that for him. His job was to study, and when there wasn't studying to be done, it was his privilege to sleep, or read, or go into town to a movie. His consuming passion was to pass the college entrance examination, and there was only one way to do it — study! So he did study, and he did pass, and the next step was the University College at Dar es Salaam, one of the three branches of the University of East Africa, the others being in Nairobi (Kenya), and Kampala (Uganda).

Dar es Salaam can be an impressive town to one used to small mud villages, or even to one who has lived in Arusha for six years. The ocean lies at its doorstep, magnificently blue, and ships from around the world tie up at its docks. There are wide tarmac roads, big buildings along Independence Avenue, imposing houses lining the roads, crowded buses, movie theaters, shops with all kinds of expensive goods, tourists with cameras hanging from their necks. The visitor immediately notices the high percentage of Asians and whites, for the city itself has only a sixty-six percent black African population, and twenty-nine percent Asians and five percent white. A wide tarmac road runs west out of town to the University College, an impressive collection of tall white buildings, built on three hills. The classroom buildings are of white concrete and glass, connected with each other by concrete walks protected from rain and sun by continuous roofs. The professors and instructors live in long red-roofed houses, with curving driveways and manicured lawns. Yonatani lived in a high-rise building which had a view of the entire campus and in the distance the city of Dar and the Indian Ocean beyond.

Quickly he began to identify with the other students. They lived in a world apart from the rest of the country. They were the elite, the cream of the crop, representing one-tenth of one percent of the student population of Tanzania.*

And they knew it. To their credit, most of them were there for the primary reason of getting a university

* In 1967 there were about 1,000 students in college, 25,000 in secondary school, 825,000 in grade school.

degree. But because of their long-time isolation from the other citizens of Tanzania, they had difficulty picturing their position in the overall view. They were impatient with everyone, argumentative both with white professors and the black man on the street. They read the *Nationalist* (organ of the one political party in Tanzania) avidly, and soon could spice an entire conversation with cliches that appeared endlessly in the paper concerning colonialism, neo-colonialism, imperialism, self-reliance for building socialism, and so forth. Yonatani soon began to realize just how shallow his thinking had been, and how badly he had been deluded by his instructors in secondary school.

Expatriates (any one who lives in Tanzania without becoming a citizen) were to be tolerated only because they brought with them some ability or knowledge which could be used by the Tanzanians to further their own knowledge of science, mathematics, architecture, physics, medicine, law, etc. But once there were trained Tanzanians to do the teaching, the expatriates must go. No longer must they be allowed to wax fat and rich from the sweat of the Africans' brows. Yonatani began to see just how far down the river he had been sold, how he had unwittingly adopted the colonial mentality without even realizing it. He considered himself fortunate to have found this out so early in his life.

He began to take a real interest in the politics of his country, and as he did so, he could literally tear to shreds the ideologies of his professors as they tried doggedly to impose on him the tenets of the Western World. He began to enjoy baiting the professors, especially the Englishmen, but also the Americans, and he would write provocative sentences on the blackboard for them to read when they came into class. The favorite topics of course were racism in the United States, English foreign policy in Rhodesia since UDI (Unilateral Declaration of Independence), the Viet Nam war, and the Cuban revolution. The day following Stokely Carmichael's lecture on the magnificence of the Cuban revolution, Yonatani left a Cuban newspaper on the desk of his educational psychology professor. He laughed to himself as he pictured the grimace that must have appeared on the professor's face when he picked up the paper.

Not that he himself was completely sold on the Castro type of socialism, but the man was a revolutionary, and that was enough to make him a hero. Yonatani also tended to identify himself with other heroes of revolutions: Patrice Lumumba, Che Guevara, Mao Tse-tung, Ho Chi Minh. He spent an unusual amount of time and energy in espousing the tenets of revolution, forgetting for the time that the Tanzanians did not get independence by bloody revolution, and perhaps this was a source of some discomfort to the young hotbloods in the University College. Perhaps they would have preferred to gain independence in some bloody conflict, rather than in the quiet, orderly way in which it had come, with hardly a ripple in the lives of anyone except the very top brass in government.

Reading the *Nationalist,* Yonatani got the distinct impression that there was one common idea in the minds of the other countries of the world, and that idea was to infiltrate, subvert, terrorize, tear down, and in other ways bring about the economic and political control of his new country. He had the feeling that this was their primary aim – they had no other problems or thoughts with which to deal. If he had thought this over, he would have seen the ridiculousness of it, but it was easier and more ego-building to consider all the countries of the world as being bent on the destruction of Tanzania. He felt, along with the *Nationalists,* that Hitler was less of a monster than the neo-colonialists who were trying to undermine and destroy Tanzania.

In August of 1967 one of his professors suggested a

debate to be concerned with the differences of education under colonialism and under the new system proposed by President Nyerere's monograph "Education for Self-reliance." The professor naively supposed that there would be two views represented in the debate, and he did not assign students to take either side. To his acute embarrassment, every student, including Yonatani, presented the colonialist's side, arguing that the old system was better than that proposed by the President. He found himself in the odd position of having to summarize the national attitudes, including the fact that the native African has one important advantage over the expatriate teacher by just being African.

After class, Yonatani argued with the professor that he had no right to take either side, and it was then that the professor noted for the first time the peculiar eyes of the student. The professor argued that he did have the right, indeed the obligation, to present the national reasoning as expressed in the Self-reliance pamphlet. He argued that Nyerere was teaching the correct things in that monograph, especially so because he went along with world-thought in his presentation. This also irritated Yonatani, and added one more reason for Yonatani to some day put the professor in his place.

The day after Stokely Carmichael spoke on the Cuban revolution, he lectured on Black Power. His special point, of course, was the oppression of blacks by whites, and his target was the U.S.A. He had a sympathetic audience until he began to criticize the disunity among the freedom fighters of Africa, and then he lost them. The following day Yonatani and his friends were of the opinion that Carmichael was not to be trusted, and they questioned his motives in coming to Africa, and wondered if he were attempting to establish a power base in Africa. Then he was forgotten.

Or almost forgotten. For there lingered an intriguing

respect and fascination for his emotion-packed statements about "containing" the white man.

When Yonatani attended his class in educational psychology that afternoon, someone had written on the blackboard, "The white man denies the Negro his rights." The professor entered the room, read the blackboard impassively, and asked if the students would like to discuss the lectures by Carmichael. The students had already caucussed in the morning and decided that it would do no real good to bring up such an inflammatory subject in the classroom, so their spokesman told the professor they would rather get on with the lesson for the day.

The class continued until about five minutes were left, and then Yonatani could stand it no longer. He had seethed during the entire morning, then during the seminar, wishing to say so many things that would put this white man in his proper place in the scheme of things, and had hardly participated in the discussion. He allowed his rage to build up, until it was no longer possible for him to think rationally. He remembered all the stories he had heard about the maltreatment of Africans under the British, and the stories he had read about the subservience of the black man in America (who after all had really built the country), and he raised his hand with five minutes of the class period left. He insisted that the professor comment on the statement on the board.

The professor stood thoughtfully for nearly a full minute, ordering his words into logical phrases so that he could explain his feelings adequately. Finally he said, "The statement implies that the white man is the keeper of the black man's rights. Too many blacks as well as whites believe this to be true. The white man does not *hold* the black man's rights, nor the black *hold* the white's anywhere."

He was about to go on, still logically, intending to tie this into a previous lecture where he had outlined the notion that teacher attitudes of superiority over pupils (and pupils' parents) was not conducive to good education; that attitudes of superiorness anywhere stultified development whether it was development of a whole ethnic group or nation or individual pupil. But he was interrupted by Yonatani, who sat near the front of the room close to the blackboard, and who reached around the professor and wrote clearly in block letters:

KILL HIM

The professor turned slowly to read the new writing, and when he turned to face the class again, they were all silently leaving.

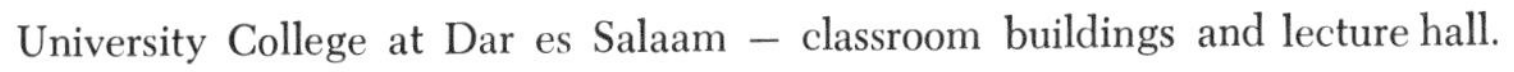

University College at Dar es Salaam – classroom buildings and lecture hall.

13 / Hospitali ya Wa-mishoneri wa Kiomboi

In the previous chapters of this book, the reader has met a couple dozen Africans from the plains around the plateau on which the author lived. He has, perhaps, begun to sense the brooding loneliness of those vast savannas, and to catch the mood of the author when he penned the poem at the beginning of this book. He may have begun to appreciate some of the problems which the men living on those plains face in their day-to-day living. He should have a little insight into tribal life. He is even starting to feel at home with the words "*boma,*" "*safari,*" "*jambo,*" and "*bwana!*"

The reader also has met the author from time to time, sharing a few of his experiences when he comes into contact with the Africans he has tried to portray, and in a few places where for a short time the author himself has become the central figure in the drama of the plains.

The time has come, now, to put the author in his place, that is, to put him back in the hospital where he was based, to find out what he was doing when he wasn't out hunting or safari-ing. Obviously, one chapter cannot reconstruct the work of three years, but it can outline some of the problems and some of the solutions.*

I do not intend this book to be a medical journal, and so far it hasn't been. But I went to Africa to deal with disease, and since many people are fascinated with medical problems, I think it only right that we terminate this book with a discussion of those problems.

An illustrative episode. It was a Sunday morning in August. The mid-winter wind whistled steadily outside the house as it does most of the time in the dry season, and I pulled the wool blankets closer around me. I had gone to bed sick and I woke up sick. Just snaking my arm out of the covers to look at my watch was enough to start the chills again, and realizing that it was already nine o'clock didn't make me feel any better. The thought crossed my mind to send a note to the hospital saying I couldn't come down, but then I remembered the woman who was scheduled for anesthesia at 10 A.M. so her fractured arm could be set. She had come in the night before, her stomach full of potatoes so that we couldn't give her a general anesthetic and the fracture too old (three days) to do it under local block.

Edna and the children were at church when I stumbled out of bed, dizzy and nauseated, dragging one leg because of a swollen knee, and found a little milk and bread to eat. The hospital seemed a mile away. When I got there I found the emergency room locked up and no one around. The surgery rooms also were empty although it was ten o'clock and people should have been there getting ready for the fracture case.

Scarcely knowing where I was or where I was going, I limped out to the wards. The medical assistants had made rounds, and I found a small list of patients at

* See footnote, page 10.

each nurses' station for me to see. A cardiac was in trouble on Ward C, female medicine, and there were a few others which I can't remember now. On the male medical ward everyone was in good condition and there was no one to examine. I sighed deeply with relief and slumped into a chair to rest for a moment.

As I made my way to the male surgical ward my head was swimming as if I had been under water too long. There were two patients to be seen. One was a patient with a distended abdomen who had been in the hospital for five days, but had been improving steadily without surgery. He was now distended again, and had not shown evidence of bowel activity for almost twenty-four hours. We knew he had taken native medicine and were watching him closely for signs of a real obstruction. Two days before, he had been seen by Dr. Burkitt (see page 188, this chapter), and he had agreed with the non-surgical treatment, so we felt we were on the right track. The decision was now mine, and I couldn't make it. The next closest surgeon was 250 miles away.

The second patient was a fifteen-year-old boy with a fracture of the leg. There was a small triangular laceration about three inches from the fracture site and the bones were obviously in poor position. It would have been a difficult decision under the best of circumstances: should it be operated upon, cleaned up, reduced into good alignment, or be left alone with just a cast? The niggling thought came to me that it should be operated upon, but then dizziness and nausea virtually exploded inside me and I knew I couldn't make the decision, nor could I even do the surgery if I decided to operate! I told the nurses to splint the leg and get an immediate X-ray. They said there was no one around to take the picture. I barked at them, "Then get someone," knowing that they wouldn't.

I literally staggered back toward surgery and found Carol Anderson, a recently arrived missionary nurse, and while I lay down in the dressing room she rounded up the people we needed to fix the wrist fracture. I slept for ten minutes or so, felt better, and rested until they called me to surgery. I set the fracture, put on a cast, and went back to the dressing room and lay down again. I didn't sleep because I kept thinking about the boy with the leg fracture, wondering if I should operate on him and knowing I couldn't. I stumbled back to my house and slept off and on the rest of the day.

The next morning I was better, still weak and woozy, but capable of making my own decisions. The compound fracture definitely should have been operated on the previous day, but the bowel obstruction was better, and the decision (if you can really call it that) not to operate was correct. There was a 50/50 chance on both, and I lost one and won one. But of course it was not I that lost or won. The young boy with the fracture was the one who lost, because his hospitalization was undoubtedly prolonged because of my inability to think straight.

This is an example of what can happen at a mission hospital when there is only one doctor. Fortunately, we usually had two doctors there, but Dr. Donald Rude was on vacation at the time of the above episode. He himself had been alone at Kiomboi for five months before I returned to Africa. The main reason I returned to Kiomboi was that I knew what was happening with Don there alone.

When there is only one doctor, something has to give. If he spends all his time in surgery, which it is possible to do, he will not be able to help screen the outpatients, nor make comprehensive ward rounds, nor do the administrative work. If, instead of operating, he spends all his time in the wards or seeing outpatients, many other patients will suffer with surgically correctable diseases. Obviously, therefore, he must compromise, and both major aspects of the hospital work get short shrift.

Furthermore, the doctor needs some time to himself, off call, once or twice a month for two or three days, and once or twice a year for one or two weeks. So I am unalterably opposed to one-doctor hospitals in developing countries, except for limited periods of time. If there must be hospitals where there is one doctor, there should be scheduled visits by other doctors who will come for a weekend to "cover" the work while the resident doctor goes hunting or just stays home and rests. It is fair neither to the doctor nor his patients to place him alone in an isolated spot for an indefinite period of time. To get this "off-call coverage," it is necessary to have some organization of the medical services, and this raises problems too complex to discuss here.

The medical problems. I am often asked what medical situations presented the biggest headaches. If I had to pick out one group of complications that vexed us the most, it would have to be obstetrical. This was partly because we had not had extensive training in "OB" but mostly because each case represented two lives that were on the brink of death. Even after almost three years of day-to-day work in obstetrics I still faced difficult labors with a certain amount of trepidation.

On the OB ward we were very often presented with truly terrifying situations – terrifying to us, to the nurses, and to the patients themselves, although the patients were so often nearly dead they didn't realize just how badly off they were. Perhaps a few illustrations would help to make the point clear.

One morning at about 4 A.M., two student nurses came to my window, scratched on the screen to wake me, and told me that a woman had just been brought to the labor ward with her baby completely delivered except for the head. I happened to have the Land-Rover at the house, so we all piled in and drove the

400 yards to the hospital. The hospital was dark, of course, since the generator was shut off at about 10:45 each night. We found our way to the labor ward with flashlights, and there we had the use of kerosene pressure lamps.

The woman was on the table, legs up in "stirrups," the baby hanging from her body. Dead. There was no heartbeat, no attempts at respirations. The cord itself was pulseless, indicating that the placenta had separated from the uterus and was lying free in the cavity. The mother had been in labor for forty-eight hours, and was comatose because she had been given no food or water during that time. She had been given liberal doses of native medicine, perhaps some uterus-stimulating drug similar to pitocin – a powerful uterine stimulant commonly used in U.S. hospitals in carefully calculated doses to initiate labor. I did a procedure which always somewhat sickens me, but it is the only thing to do in such situations when the baby is dead: I transected the neck of the baby, reached up into the uterus with artery forceps and turned the head so that it would deliver easily. The mother revived readily with the proper fluids given intravenously, and left the hospital in a few days.

On another occasion I was called to see a new admission who had been in labor for over five days. The baby had lain in a transverse position so that when labor started the arm came out first, locking the head high in the uterus. The baby had been dead for at least two days, the arm grossly swollen, purple, and gangrenous. The mother was unconscious, so without anesthesia I amputated the baby's arm with two quick snips of the scissors, slipped my fingers up into the uterus and quite easily extracted the baby feet first. This mother also survived, and went home after about ten days.

Sometimes the girls came to us at the first sign of trouble and we still had problems. One young girl, pregnant for the first time, came to us with a history of minor bleeding off and on for about a week. She was almost ready to go into labor, so we admitted her for observation. We drew blood from all her friends and relatives and obtained two pints which were compatible with her blood. With this security we waited.

A week went by, and she didn't bleed at all. During the second week she "spotted" a little each day, and then finally went into labor. She progressed slowly, but finally delivered a normal baby and all of us relaxed. Prematurely. The placenta failed to deliver. We waited an hour, an hour and a half, and then she started to bleed slowly. We made preparations to remove the placenta manually, started blood in the intravenous that we had already introduced, and just as I began to go after the placenta she gushed forth about a pint of blood in one big push. I extracted the placenta in just a few seconds, and she immediately stopped bleeding. This was one of the more rewarding cases, although we felt as if we were sitting on a powder keg for the entire two weeks before delivery.

In all likelihood the above case would have been operated upon much sooner if she had been here in the United States. The entire philosophy of Cesarean sections is different in Africa. Too many of our patients would fail to return for succeeding deliveries, and too many would rupture their uteruses out in the bush, so we avoided "C-sections" if there was any other way to get the baby out alive. These other procedures included operations on the bones of the pelvis to enlarge the birth canal (symphysiotomies), a procedure roundly condemned in the States but widely used and highly praised in Africa.

Sometimes we lost both baby and mother. A woman came in late one night after a three-day labor. She had been given large doses of kerosene by mouth, a rather common treatment in our area, and was very toxic. The baby was still alive, but the fluid draining from the uterus was darkly stained with feces from the baby's intestinal tract, indicating severe deprivation of oxygen. We rushed the mother to the operating room and did a Cesarean section, only to find a lifeless infant. It had died in the few moments it had taken us to get ready for the operation. I performed mouth-to-mouth resuscitation, then passed a catheter into the child's trachea and ventilated the lungs while Daudi Mzengi, our head OR nurse, gave external cardiac massage. After twenty minutes it was obvious we had a dead baby, and after thirty minutes we discontinued our efforts. The mother lived for almost three weeks, a vegetable, then died from severe kerosene poisoning of the lungs, kidneys and brain.

A fifteen-year-old Sukuma girl came in with her first baby jammed into the pelvis, four days after labor had started. The mother seemed in good condition, and, surprisingly, so was the baby, even though the head was almost to the outlet. She was so close to delivery that I watched her very carefully for a short while, hoping she would continue. After two hours it was obvious nothing was happening, so I did a symphysiotomy and the baby almost shot out, squalling and yelling its little head off. He seemed to be saying, "It's about time you got me out of there!"

I could go on and on with stories about triumphs and failures, but perhaps one more incident will be enough. Again it was about 4 A.M., the kerosene lamps throwing shadows on the walls as the nurses moved around the room. I was sitting on a revolving stool, watching one of our midwives, Fredaeli Oforo, doing a breech delivery. The midwives did all of the completely normal deliveries, calling us at the first (and least) sign of any trouble. We insisted that they always call us for breech deliveries, but we often allowed them to handle the case in our presence unless there was trouble. They did a good job, and since many of them would be going on to other clinics or isolated dispensaries where they would *have* to do this kind of work on their own, we felt they should have the experience of doing complicated cases when help was immediately available.

In this particular case, things went very well. Miss Oforo took the infant gently in her hands, directing the body downwards with very gentle traction until the head rotated, then gradually lifting upward and outward, watching the woman's perineum for signs of rupture (in which case an "episiotomy" would have to be done – a small incision in the tissues to allow more room), then lowering the baby's body again to see if the head was ready to clear the pubic bones, raising the body again when she saw that it wasn't quite ready, then, when the baby's mouth was at the mother's anus, lowering the baby again until it slipped out.

Well done, I thought, and said it aloud. But the mother's abdomen was still very large. I felt of it and told the mother that there was another one still inside. She cried out in joy and obvious embarrassment. The nurses laughed and joked with her: to the women in our area twins are no longer thought to be due to witchcraft (so that one or both must be destroyed), but are considered an indisputable sign of great fertility, perhaps the single most important attribute of a woman. It was a happy occasion, especially when the second baby delivered normally shortly thereafter, and helped to make up for all the horrible things we saw in that same room before and after that night.

Next in line to the obstetrical problems were the diseases of the female reproductive organs. Taking first honors in the headache department were the "fistulas," holes between the vagina and the bladder or the rectum, most commonly caused by prolonged labors with the head of the baby causing such pressure on the structures in the pelvis that the tissues actually slough away, leaving direct communications between the pelvic organs. These patients are probably the most miserable people in the world. If the fistula is between the bladder and the vagina, urine runs continuously down the legs without any way for the woman to control it. Similarly, if the fistula is to the rectum, feces are uncontrollable. Some women have both, but the more common is the bladder-vagina fistula. In either case, the woman is socially unacceptable, even in primitive areas where earthy odors are not as repugnant as they are to us.

I did see one exception to this, however, in a woman who had a small fistula to the bladder. She became pregnant and we had to do a Cesarean section to prevent further breakdown. A few months later we operated on her to correct the fistula — both operations were successful. Unfortunately not all of our repairs held, and repeat operations were sometimes necessary. This is hard on both doctor and patient! Occasionally there was literally no tissue left at the base of the bladder, where the muscular control of urination lies, and we had to resort to transplanting the ureters (tubes leading from kidneys to bladder) into the bowel, and then these presented problems of their own.

More common than the fistulas were uterine tumors and gonorrheal diseases of the tubes. Oftentimes the pelvis was converted to a mass (mess?) of enlarged and inflamed tubes encased in old scar tissue which smoldered for months and years, causing continuous pain until the entire pelvis was cleaned out surgically. Some of my most grateful patients were those who had borne pain for years, not knowing that surgical help was possible, then came to the hospital where we were able to solve their problem for them.

On the male side, we dealt with the whole gamut of surgical problems that are seen in the States. They ranged from hernia to peptic ulcer to obstructions of the urinary tract from prostate enlargement or gonorrhea, but our most common problem was the giant leg ulcer. Originating from a small thorn prick or infected cut, it spreads outwards in a matter of days, sometimes involving the entire lower leg. After early treatment with hot packs and antibiotics, we were uniformly successful in curing the ulcer by first excising it in its entirety at one operation, then skin-grafting the healthy granulation tissues (proud flesh) about a week later. In this particular disease we dealt with basically healthy tissues under the ulcers, a situation not often found in the States, where ulcers are usually due to poor circulation.

The problems of untrained ancillary personnel. In general surgery we faced several formidable handicaps, not the least of which was anesthesia. Both Dr. Rude and I had had some training in anesthesia, but it is difficult to be both surgeon and anesthetist, and if we both were in the OR at the same time a lot of other work just didn't get done. So we compromised. We did everything possible under spinal anesthesia, which enabled the surgeon to first give the anesthetic, then to do the operation while a nurse monitored the blood pressure and pulse.

Whenever the operation involved the head, neck, or chest, we would give the anesthetic for the other doctor, which of course tied both of us up for the duration of that case, but this was only necessary once or twice a month. We were also training Daudi Mzengi, our OR supervisor, to give general anesthesia, and he was coming along well enough that he could handle the course of an uncomplicated case quite well. But when he was giving an anesthetic, he was withdrawn from the nursing end of the operation and this was not good either because we needed him to handle the many nursing problems that arose in the OR.

A second major problem was finding adequate surgical assistance at the operating table. We tried using the medical assistants, and they were good, but when they were in the OR they could not be in the out-patient department, and this slowed down the operation of the entire hospital. Again we compromised. We routinely used a graduate nurse as a first assistant, only calling on a medical assistant to help if the case promised to be a particularly difficult one.

I don't think the importance of good assistance is generally appreciated by the lay public. The best assistant is usually a good surgeon himself, because he knows what the surgeon is going to do next, and he anticipates his moves, holding tissues or instruments in just the proper manner so that the surgeon can work at his optimum speed and efficiency. Nothing slows down a surgeon more than having to repeatedly direct the retraction of muscles or the placing of hemostats or the tying of knots. A good assistant can literally make a good surgeon out of a mediocre one by judicious movements or comments and can prevent errors in technique which might jeopardize the outcome of the entire case. I know. I have been on both sides of the table.

I remember one morning when I was fortunate in not losing my mind completely. Everything went wrong. A young African lad had come to us for a month between his first and second year of medical assistant's training. He was a bright young man, anxious to please, but he just hadn't had the background for moving into the operating theater. If he had told me beforehand, I would have coached him, and would have started him on a simpler case, but he said he knew all the ground rules about getting ready for assisting at an operation.

I watched him out of the corner of my eye as he got ready. He contaminated himself four times, necessitating re-scrubbing each time. Twice he broke technique with the towel while he dried his hands, and once he reached around to help the nurse tie his gown, and the last time he put on the sterile gloves in a very poor manner. Finally he was ready. I was doing a tough fracture case, an old both-bone fracture of the forearm which was shortened and full of scar tissue. At one point I clamped a large blood vessel, handed him the clamp to hold while I tied it, and he proceeded to take the clamp off too soon, blood shooting all over the sterile drapes. Reacting quickly, before I could, he jabbed the hemostat down into the wound to catch the bleeder, and narrowly missed the radial nerve which if clamped would have caused paralysis and loss of sensation in a large part of the hand. I excused him at that point! He left in mortification, which I hated to see, but I just couldn't risk any more troubles.

As it turned out, I had enough of my own that had nothing to do with my assistant. First, the nurses had forgotten to sterilize bone-holding forceps, so we waited another ten minutes while they were sterilized. Then when we had gotten the metal rods in place I found that there were no extractors to move them into better position. About that time the circulating nurse, who is supposed to be available in the OR at all times, disappeared, and we couldn't find anyone to get some sterile roller gauze to complete the case. I retired to the dressing room, put my feet up on the table, and sipped on some hot coffee from the thermos I had brought down with me in the early morning. I must admit I dreamed a little of home.

Death in the Operating Room. Sometimes the cases were just too tough for us to pull out. An old man came in late one afternoon with the story that he had swallowed a fish bone the day before and it had gotten stuck in his throat. His sons had poked sticks in his mouth and had dug with their fingers, but they had gotten nowhere. He had a foul-smelling mouth, with rotten craggy teeth. His mouth would not open because of inflammation and swelling in the jaws and the neck. I suspected that his sons had perforated his throat.

We put him to sleep and then I could open his mouth a little, far enough to look at the voice-box and throat. There was nothing there except deep cuts from the sticks and fingernails of his sons. I passed a tube into his upper esophagus and found it completely filled with rotting half-chewed fish. I worked for about an hour clearing out the debris, and when I was just about done, his heart stopped and we could not revive him. He was almost awake at the time of the cardiac arrest, so I feel he wasn't anesthetized too deeply, but I suspect the trauma and irritation of his lower esophagus caused reflex stoppage of the heart. At any rate, we lost him.

Almost the same thing happened to a young baby who had gotten a piece of a pumpkin seed in his trachea. He had been treated for pneumonia in the pediatrics ward for three days before we awoke to the fact that he had aspirated a foreign body. We had thought he was too young to have gotten anything solid into his lungs, but the mother finally admitted that she had been feeding him pumpkin and it was "possible that he had swallowed a seed." We put him to sleep, a hazardous procedure under the best of circumstances, and I slipped a bronchoscope down into his trachea. I got the seed out all right, but it took a long time, and I had been unable to watch the condition of the patient during that time. When the seed and bronchoscope were safely out, I found that the baby was no longer breathing. We tried everything we could think of to revive him, but he was dead.

It was twelve noon on a Saturday, several years ago now, but I remember in vivid detail everything I did, everything I said, and the chilling tragedy of it is still with me.

Non-surgical pediatric problems. In general, our

pediatric problems were not surgical, although as you have just seen, some of them were, and they could be tough. The main reason, however, for admission to the pediatric ward was malaria and its complications. Some of our babies were born with malaria and began showing signs of fever and poor feeding habits as early as the first few days of life, but the most serious cases were those from six months to a year old. Our diagnosis was often "malaria and pneumonia," but whether the malaria or pneumonia came first I don't know, and it doesn't make any difference to the baby or to the doctor because the treatment is the same. A dreaded complication was "cerebral malaria," infestation so overwhelming that the brain was swollen to the point of causing coma, convulsions, and often death.

One of the more interesting, but tragic, problems with which we dealt was a cancer of children called "Burkitt's Lymphoma," described by Dr. Denis Burkitt* in 1962. The tumor occurs in equatorial Africa at altitudes ranging from 3000 to 5000 feet, and involves the faces of the children in grotesque ways. Sometimes the tumor arises behind the eye and causes horrible protrusions of the eyeball. Occasionally it arises on both sides of the face, producing a bilaterally symmetrical swelling of the jaws or cheeks. Always we found evidence in the body of other tumors, indicating that it was a multiple cancer which showed up most dramatically in the face and neck.

Fortunately there was a drug which often caused rapid regression of the tumors, and in Dr. Burkitt's series he has a high percentage of actual "cures." The drug is methotrexate, a highly toxic cellular poison, so it must be given in carefully measured dosages according to the weight of the patient.

* See *Today's Health,* Sept., 1968, or the condensation in *Readers Digest,* also Sept., 1968 (Dr. Burkitt Tracks a Cancer Clue), or *Mr. Burkitt and Africa,* a book by Bernard Glemser (World Publishing Company, 1970).

Dr. Burkitt visited us for two days at Kiomboi, staying in our home, and we were able to obtain a great deal of personal insight into the problems of this particular disease, as well as help in other areas, for Dr. Burkitt has spent a lifetime working with tropical diseases of all kinds. He is a quiet, unassuming Irishman, speaks softly with a faint lisp, and has the brain of a clinical researcher. He continually asks himself the question "why" when presented with a problem, and it was this inquisitiveness that led him on the search for the clue to the cancer of children which has come to bear his name. He carried this attitude into all the aspects of his practice, at one point shocking the nurses (and me), when we were making ward rounds, by asking, "Do you still take the temperature, pulse, and respirations of *all* your patients four times a day? It's ridiculous! It wastes the nurses' time, it irritates the patients, and even more importantly it isn't necessary in more than 5-10 percent of the cases. Take the temperature *once* a day, in the evening, unless you *really* want to know if there is a pattern of fever, then order it specifically." This was typical of his drive for perfection, and this drive included the eliminating of unnecessary motions.

Other medical problems. In the previous pages we have touched on some of the problems with which we were faced daily. There were many others: fractures, ruptured tubal pregnancies, congenital defects in children, animal injuries (at one time or another I treated injuries caused by hyena, leopard, lion, snake, buffalo, and even an old arm injury by a rhino), bowel obstruction, ruptured spleens, cancer (in just about every organ), eye diseases (especially trachoma, injuries, and foreign bodies), abdominal tumors of frequently giant proportions, and many others.

The hospital personnel. When I tell people that our

OPD (Outpatient Department) tended to the ills of 1000 patients a day, the immediate reaction is unbelief. It is true. In fact, there were many days when 1200-1300 patients were registered and seen in the OPD. How did we do it?

The answer is two-fold: organization, and medical assistants.

The OPD was undoubtedly the best organized part of our hospital. Patients were seen first by a senior nurse, who directed them to the injection room, the "ulcer room," the treatment room, the consultation rooms of the medical assistants, the doctor, a hospital ward, the laboratory, X-ray, pharmacy, or special clinic. The medical assistants screened all new patients, directing them to the proper place in the hospital, or prescribing treatment for them on the spot. Perhaps about five percent of the patients were seen by the doctor on any given day, the rest having been taken care of by the medical assistants or the nurses. I have often said, and there can be no doubt it is an understatement, that our hospital could not have functioned without the medical assistants.

Who were these medical assistants? They were young men who had had high academic standing in their high schools and who were sent on to a three-year medical course specializing in, but not limited to, diseases of the tropics, so that when they came to us they were well-versed in most of the diseases they would see. They were also well-enough grounded in non-tropical diseases that they could differentiate between tropical and non-tropical problems, and treat most of them. If they were in doubt at all, they referred the patient to the doctor. Unfortunately, when we doctors were in doubt, we had no such easy out!

The system needs no defense. It worked. *Res ipsa loquitur.* The thing speaks for itself.

Similarly, the hospital could not have functioned without our African nurses. We employed an average of twenty-five nurses, graduates of our own nursing school. The average education was eight years of grade school and three years of nurses' training. These girls (and boys) were skilled in the practical aspects of nursing care, and with proper guidance could usually be counted on to deliver adequate care to their patients. Some were outstanding, and these people were singled out to be sent to bigger medical centers for further training as soon as space and funds became available. About a half dozen of our nurses had taken "upgrading" courses which qualified them as Grade A nurses, roughly equivalent to the standards set for graduates of our schools in the States.

I might say, parenthetically, that the general care of patients by the nurses had improved considerably between my first and second tour of duty at Kiomboi. The primary reason was, of course, that they all had had an additional four years of experience in hospital work, and a higher percentage had received the upgrading training that I mentioned above. There was the added incentive of working in their "own" hospital. When I was first there, I could sense that many of the nurses felt they were working in a foreigner's mission hospital, the key posts occupied by missionaries, whereas during my second tour there was the definite feeling among the personnel that they were working in their own hospital, with most of the important jobs held by their own people. They had a "stake" in what was happening, and they had the say in what was going on. This attitude was not universal, and I was often frustrated by what I considered improper motivation, with too much emphasis on an eight-hour day, but anyone who has worked in Stateside hospitals will immediately recognize that this is not a special prerogative of the African nurse!

Finances. The economics of our hospital will interest many readers. Our annual budget for 1968 came to

Shillings 532,890 ($76,127, of which $22,400 came as a direct grant from the Church Mission Board in the States, and $50,440 came as a direct grant from the Tanzania Government). The remaining monies came from several sources. From this budget were paid all the operating expenses of the hospital including salaries (but excluding missionaries' salaries, which came from the Mission Board).

Remembering that the minimum monthly wage for the country, set by the Federal Government, is $18, it might be interesting to tabulate a sampling of the salaries paid to our hospital personnel.

Medical assistant (11 yr. experience)	$100 per month
Medical assistant (5 yr. experience)	85
Staff nurse (A) (3 yr. experience)	58
Staff nurse (A) (1 yr. experience)	52
Staff nurse (B) (8 yr. experience)	52
Staff nurse (B) (5 yr. experience)	50
Staff nurse (B) (1 yr. experience)	43
Nurse-midwife (8 yr. experience)	50
Chief maintenance man	93
Chief cook	58
Clerk to adm. assist.	26
OPD clerk	22
Laundry worker	20
Caretaker grounds	18
Assist. cook	18
Kitchen aid	18

It is interesting to read these salaries in the light of the fact that the average per capita monthly income in Tanzania is about $5. It is not difficult to see why a position in any capacity in a hospital is so desirable. The fact remains, of course, that the African family *can* exist without any cash income, or very little. The only expense the tribal African has is the yearly "head tax," which varies from region to region but is approximately $3-5. This can be raised by selling a goat or a sheep, or by working for wages in the nearest village or town for five to ten days during the year, or in several other ways. There is no tax on the land, no rent since he builds his own house, no food to buy since he can raise or find his own, skins to use for clothes if he wants nothing better, etc.

The average African nowadays, of course, does not dress in skins, nor does he raise all his food, and he is desirous of obtaining some of the *accoutrements* of better living such as kitchenware, furniture, radios, bicycles, wristwatches, and so forth, so he is anxious to improve his lot by having a steady income. In the pure tribal society, this is difficult if not impossible, so he seeks employment on a regular basis, and he knows that the higher his education the higher will be his income. This is common sense and it has not been lost on the African.

The role of the mission hospital. Although this book is not an apologia on mission work, I would like to answer two questions I am frequently asked.

"Just what is the mission hospital doing in Tanzania these days?"

And the corollary question, "How long will the mission hospital stay in Tanzania?"

The function of the mission hospital has not changed. There may be gradually changing emphases, but the three aspects are still there: service, witness, and evangelism.

First and foremost, there must be a continuing *service* by missionary doctors and nurses, a service to be continued until the local people have produced sufficient quantity and quality of trained personnel to guarantee uninterrupted medical care to the people of the area in which the medical facility is located.

Likewise, there must be a continuing *witness* of the Christian church by the personnel of the hospital. This function was once the prerogative of the missionaries, since they were the only Christians in their area, but slowly this has changed to the point where they are in a minority; that is, the majority of Christians are now native Africans, and it is upon these African Christians that the major witness devolves. The missionary Christians and the African Christians now have a wonderful opportunity to work together on the same projects, demonstrating for all to see the peace, harmony and unifying love of Christ. They can, together, demonstrate clearly that Christ's love works in them, controls them, and admonishes them daily to show mercy to the sick in His name. The success of their witness will be in direct proportion to their ability to do this.

Evangelism in mission hospitals has followed two routes, depending more often on the desires and abilities of the medical personnel than on any church policy. Put more bluntly, the "spreading of the Gospel" will, in some cases, be done primarily by the doctors and nurses (foreign or native), whereas in other cases the work of evangelism will be done primarily by the African minister in the local church or an African chaplain assigned directly to the hospital. If the doctor or nurse is evangelically oriented and motivated, and has the time, and is capable of speaking the language of the people, he or she may spend hours talking with individual patients or actually preaching sermons in the wards or in the OPD.

Most doctors and nurses (foreign and native) have neither the time nor the inclination to do this, so what usually happens is that the evangelistic mission of the church is carried out by pastors. Before native pastors were trained, this was done by missionary pastors, but now the work is almost uniformly done by local people. At our hospital the pastor of the Kiomboi Church spent a great deal of time at the hospital, counseling and comforting those already Christian and preaching to the non-Christian patients.

The second question – how long the mission hospitals will stay in Tanzania – has been partly answered already. They will remain mission hospitals as long as there is need for missionary personnel to staff them, and perhaps even longer. In India, for example, there are few places where foreign doctors are still needed to carry on the practice of medicine, and many hospitals once fully staffed by missionaries now have only Indian doctors on the staff. Some of these are still partly subsidized by mission funds, whereas others have been turned over to the government.*

But I think it is clear in Tanzania, to all who can read the signs, that the missionary doctors who make up nearly one hundred percent of the medical staffs of the fifty mission hospitals in that country, will only be allowed to continue their work as long as there are not enough Africans to do the job. This may be twenty years or longer (the Tanzanians say ten), but it will come. And I should hasten to add, this is not only inevitable but good.

"Africanization" of the churches has already taken place, and there is no logical reason why Africanization of the hospitals should not also occur. Indeed, it has already happened in nursing. The outlook for mission hospitals in Tanzania is, therefore, not grim, but promising. We will have accomplished what we set out to do: to perform a service for the people while witnessing to our Savior and spreading the Gospel of Love *until such time* as they can raise up their own doctors and prophets to do the same (or better) job. Those of us who are interested enough in missions to have gone

* E.g., Rainy Hospital in Madras, where I was born, and which I visited in Dec., 1968, is still considered a mission hospital but is fully staffed by Indian doctors and nurses.

out there must have the wisdom to know when our work is done.

Yes, the work of the missionary is changing. He is no longer "sent" by the church in America, but is "called" by the church in Africa. At times this distinction may be blurred, but for the most part it is real, and it takes a different kind of person to be effective on the mission field these days than it did twenty or thirty years ago. The emphasis is on working "with," or "for," the African people, which implies a humility Christians like to talk about but find it difficult to put into practice. The emphasis is, more than ever before, on getting to know just what it is that the African wants to accomplish, and, within the bounds of the combined skill and ability of the missionary and the African, going ahead and getting the job done.

Bishop Stephano Moshi, speaking to new missionaries at an orientation conference in Dodoma, said, "You have been called by the African Church. You are our assistants. We thank you for coming with your skills, but are you skilled enough to share your knowledge with us? Are you patient with a man who might not have had the same educational advantages you have had? Humility is an adjective you can always attach to a successful missionary."

The problem comes to a head, of course, when the African and the missionary disagree on a fundamental point. The African says, "I am right. I know my people. This is the way we must go." He may even imply that the missionary is no longer in charge and so there should not even be an argument. The missionary says, "But the way you want to go is bound to fail. Let me show you why." And he may imply that even though he is no longer in charge, he does have superior wisdom and insight and has been sent out to help prevent grave errors in policy.

At this point we have an impasse. The solving of this impasse has been the subject of entire books, and I will not attempt to deal with the subject here. However, I do recall seeing the following prayer above the desk of Nurse in Charge Jean Mykelbust* at Kiomboi: "God, give me the *serenity* to accept the things I cannot change, *courage* to change what I can, and the *wisdom* to know the difference."

I would like to paraphrase that prayer so that it more accurately reflects the petition of a modern missionary in a foreign country.

"God, give me the *serenity* to accept the things with which I do not agree but which are perfectly satisfactory in *this* culture, *courage* to change what I feel would be wrong in *any* culture, and the *wisdom* to know the difference."

* Since this was written, Miss Mykelbust developed a rapidly fatal pneumonia. She was buried in the Kiomboi Church cemetery, across the sand road from her small house. Her funeral was attended by hundreds of the local people, great and small, who had known and loved her.

Mr. Marko Shila — senior nurse at Kiomboi Lutheran Hospital.

Glossary

acacia – an umbrella-shaped tree, common to the savannas of Africa

Bantu – black Africans of the Negroid race, in tropical Africa

baobab – giant tree with large trunks, small branches, which reportedly live two or three thousand years

Barabaig – tribe of pastoral people in the Great Rift Valley, near Singida, closely related to the Masai

Baraband – a male of the Barabaig tribe

boma – enclosure around a house for domestic animals. When capitalized, the seat of government for an area

breech – in obstetrics, being born buttocks-first

bronchoscope – a thin, long, end-lighted tube for looking down in the windpipe and bronchial tubes

bwana – sir, mister, master

bustard – goose-sized bird, but with crane-like legs

caldera – extinct volcano whose top has caved in

caucasoid – resembling Caucasians (Whites, Arabs, Asiatic Indians)

cornea – the tough, transparent covering of the front of the eye

dawa ya wenyeji – literally "medicine of the inhabitants," or native medicine

dik-dik – tiny antelope, weighing 10-12 pounds

eland – giant antelope, averaging 1200-1500 pounds, excellent for eating

eviscerate – to lose the contents of
euphorbia – peculiar tree which resembles a giant cactus

feces – solid waste of bowel
fici – hyena

gani – what kind of? As in "shida gani" – what kind of trouble (are you having)

hemostat – a clamp for catching bleeding vessels
Hodi – standard greeting from outside a house or room, meaning "Anyone home, may I come in?"
hospitali – hospital

impala – deer-sized antelope, with bright red coat and spiralling horns
Iramba – tribe of 150,000 farming people in which the Kiomboi Lutheran Mission Hospital is situated
Isanzu – tribe of farming people, closely akin to the Irambas in customs, bordering Iramba-land on the northeast

Jambo – hello. Literally means "Thing," shortened by long usage from "Si jambo baya?" (There is nothing wrong?)

kanga – wild guinea fowl, widespread in forest and plains, sometimes in flocks of many dozens
kanzu – a long, white, gown-like robe
Karibu – welcome, come in. Literally means "near" or "close," shortened by long usage from "Njoo karibu" (Come near). Karibuni – used for two or more persons
Kilimanjaro – 20,000 foot high mountain in northeast Tanzania, snow-covered the year around, literally means "shining mountain"
Kindira – range of mountains along Lake Eyasi, in which live the Wakindiga people
Kiomboi – village where hospital compound is located, in north central Tanzania
kwale – partridge-like bird of woodlands of East Africa

Mang'ati – term used derisively by surrounding tribes for the Barabaig people. Literally means "the enemy."
Masai – a large tribe of primitive, pastoral nomads, straddling the Kenya-Tanzania border
mbuga – open plains, savanna

Mbulu – large tribe living between Kiomboi and Masai-land
meninga – hard termite-resistant wood, often used for furniture
moran – young warrior of the Masai tribe

panga – machete, used for farming and protection
perineum – the tissues lying between the vagina and the anus
placenta – afterbirth
pori – wilderness

shida – trouble
shilling – East African currency, worth about 15 cents
shuka – wrap-around dress of most East African women
siafu – large, biting ant
Swahili – the lingua franca of East Africa, with some usage in parts of neighboring countries, spoken by perhaps fifty million people. Often seen written "Kiswahili," the "Ki" being merely the Swahili prefix meaning "language of"
symphysiotomy – operation to cut the fibrous union of the pubic bones, just above the genitalia, to enlarge the birth canal in difficult labors.

tarmac – blacktop road
Tommy – Thomson's gazelle
topi – a reddish-brown antelope of the savannas
trachoma – bacterial infection of the underside of the eyelids

uji – thin gruel of millet or corn, standard East African breakfast
ujamaa – literally means family-hood, used now in connection with communal villages
ugale – thick, mush-like food made of millet or corn, standard East African supper

wa-mishoneri – the missionaries
wattle – thin saplings and branches used in house construction
Wazungu – literally means European, actually used for all white people

DATE DUE
